Venice
An architectural guide

Guido Zucconi

Venice
An architectural guide

with an essay by
Donatella Calabi

arsenale et editrice

Guido Zucconi
VENICE
AN ARCHITECTURAL GUIDE

Design
Michela Scibilia

Translation
Antony Shugaar
Alexandra Gate (Calabi's text)

Printed in Italy by
EBS Editoriale Bortolazzi-Stei
Verona

First edition
June 1993

ISBN 88-7743-130-X

The publisher wishes to express his
thanks to all of the following for
kindly lending their photographs
Donatella Calabi
Edilvenezia SpA
Valeriano Pastor
Mark Smith
The publisher would also like to thank
the following local authorities for
having kindly authorised the taking of
pictures of the buildings under their
jurisdiction
Amministrazione Provinciale of
Venice
Direzione Musei Civici of Venice
Unità Sanitaria Locale n. 16
Venice

Authorisation for the publication of the
facsimiles of documents at the Venice
State Archives no. 24/1993.
The documents were reproduced by the
Photocopying Department of the Venice
State Archives.

Contents

Donatella
Calabi

An Itinerary through the History of the Town and its Architecture

1. For centuries, in describing the town of Venice observers generally noticed its specific nature, dwelling in particular upon the manner in which it was built on water.

In 1267 the chronicler Martino da Canal pointed to the fact that the settlement rises "upon the sea-shore, with the salty waters running through it, round it and everywhere in it, except for inside the houses and streets," so that its inhabitants always have two choices for moving about the town: on foot or by boat (fig. 2). In 1495 the French ambassador Philippe de Commynes gave vent to his bewilderment in seeing so many steeples, monasteries and buildings on water, with galleys sailing past them (fig. 1). But even a more or less contemporary (1502) native of Venice, the official historian of the Republic, Marc'Antonio Sabellico, spoke in similar terms in describing the town's origins. "It is bathed by the sea waves not just on one side, as in many other towns, but is placed in the midst of the waters;" hence, it is "more conveniently reached by sea than by land." Little over sixty years later, in describing the "extremely beautiful and singular" Venice, Francesco Sansovino looks to its fragments (the islands) and declares that "when leaving a quarter and entering another" it is as though one were going from one town into an entirely different one; this is a matter of convenience and pride for its inhabitants and a source of astonishment for foreigners (fig. 11).

In 1786 a most experienced traveller, the German poet Wolfgang Goethe, looks at it from the heights of a steeple and realizes how dynamic is the balance between the land above the sea-level and the one below; everywhere, he sees the mainland advancing where previously there had only been a large sheet of water, a wide grey-

7

2.
Anonymous
The Lagoon and City of Venice with its Network of Canals, XVIIIth century.
Venice, State Archives.

3.
Ignazio Danti
Venetia Civitas Admirabilis, about 1550.
Close-up view showing the islands of Torcello, San Francesco and Burano.
Rome, Vatican Museums.

green swamp intersected by canals (fig. 4). Lastly, Taine, in 1864 noticed its "churches and palaces that grow larger and larger and hover over the sea like spectres."

These are precise as well as suggestive literary observations which, however, are made by bewildered observers seeking the unique magic of a town that is unlike any other. They all seem to take more of an interest in the morphology of the lagoon, in the shape of the settlement, than in its individual parts. 16th and 17th century map-makers, which deeply influenced travel descriptions, often present us with the global image of a thick stone jungle entirely surrounded by the lagoon. Northern-European atlases for example, have induced us to "see" the city profile and plan in a certain way. In the former, steeples rise, just like the towers of the enceinte of Nürnberg and Lübeck, slender and sharp, towering above an indistinct mass of buildings (fig. 5). In the latter, the density of the constructions is represented by a patch, whose shape emerges uniformly from the lagoon only to be interrupted by the winding course of the river running through it, making it resemble a fish with an "S"-shaped backbone (fig. 8). Apart from the above, we also have a few descriptions of the Grand Canal as a "curtain" or "face" of buildings. The innermost part of the town's urban fabric can be visualised by adding to these general images an interpretation that pays greater heed to spatial, as opposed to temporal, succession.

An observing eye is lured by Luca Carlevarijs' engravings on the most remarkable edifices of the city, by Antonio Visentini's relief drawings, marked by a great inventiveness, or by the more precise ones made by Leopoldo Cicognara with some students of the Accademia: the view is broken up into these peculiar and isolated individual items of architecture. It no longer offers global pictures, but rather is devided into accomplished fragments which may relate to the urban unity to which they belong (the point of the customs-house, the intricate network of open spaces surrounding Saint Mark's, the island of Rialto) (fig. 7).

2. In a way, the choice made by this guide-book is rather similar. Seeing Venice without falling prey to its myths and picturesque aspects, requires a selection of the most essential buildings. In order to transcend rhetorical clichés and banality, one must proceed analytically along the path of one's field of investigation – the urban fabric, in this case – so as to produce a communicative instrument for its comprehension. In other words, one must return to the cultural age and ambience in which each of its individual components was perfected. Yet, the very notion of a

"guide-book" of a town implies a practical, and often homogeneous, approach. One must therefore analyse the object through a magnifying glass and harness all of one's summarizing skills, almost as if laying down the headwords of a dictionary. Yet one must also avoid resorting to narrative emphasis so as not to describe Venice's architecture like that of any other town. What must be made is an effort at classifying items systematically and comprehensively within the bounds of pre-established limits: the guide-book's aim of being simple must not be forsaken. The book's eight chapters have therefore been developed on the basis of an arduous interlacement of stylistic and chronological scanning processes. In each chapter the choice of the edifices to be described has been made with philological rigour, selecting the ones most relevant, from an architectural point of view, to the chosen theme, so that there may be a precise interaction between the theme and the building selected. Thus, the title of each chapter is illustrated by the index of its files. This guide-book makes no concession to effective descriptions and to colourful notes; it makes no reference to feasts, popular traditions and legends (which already play too great a part in most tourist literature on Venice); it does not linger on Venetian curiosities, on its hidden or esoteric aspects, to which an entire literary strain has been devoted. All of this is implicitly and disdainfully rejected.

3. The result is therefore a guide-book that is far from lenient with its reader, leaving, as it does, no room for narration and redundancy. Its aim is not to present him with considerations, suggestions or cues for fantasizing, but rather to provide him with precise information and knowledge. It is a simple tool, with no intention of replacing the works of scholars on parts of the town and its monuments, nor the monographs of famous architects. Quite to the contrary, it aims at helping anyone interested not merely in seeing the main buildings, but also in learning their history by looking it up where it is reported extensively – in other words, this guide-book lists all major bibliographical sources for further reference. A most judicious guide-book therefore, which, however, does not exhaust its subject-matter, but rather, which contains all the indications a curious visitor may need in order to dwell more deeply on whatever strikes his fancy or arouses his interest. The files on each edifice contain singular information on each of the stages of the building's construction without making any digressions and avoiding the kind of personification of the town and of its most celebrated edifices which has become famous in the works of the greatest writers. These files certainly do not

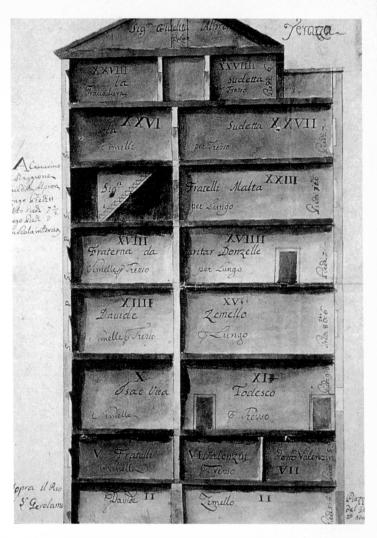

4.
XVIIIth century
drawing of the section
of a nine-floor house
overlooking the area
of the Ghetto Nuovo.
Venice, State Archives.

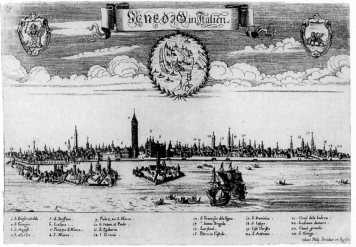

5. J.Ph. Steüdner
*Perspective View of the
City*, end-seventeenth
century.
Venice, Library of Civic
Museums.

describe Santa Maria della Salute as it was depicted by Joseph Heintz in the canvas shown on this page (fig. 6) and, several years later, by Henry James, who saw it in the guise of a grand lady in her seat, hefty and serene before her front door. They highlight its central plan design, having a continuous deambulatory, borrowed from protochristian examples; they compel one to note an added peristyle formed by two semicircular apses, or the shift from an octagon- to a round-shaped dome. Similarly, they do not speak of the palaces which "endow the Grand Canal with an air of greatness," like "disfigured and dishonoured" lords whose faces bear the unequivocal traces of age and of the passing-by of generations. They simply refer to their two- or three-bodied plans, to the wings that have been added to the initial design, with mullioned windows having many lights, with *serliane* and arched windows (fig. 9). The guide-book's theme is thus quite precise: the history of architectures – it does not even mention the works of art that are to be found therein.

Inevitably, this book pays the price of a bibliography which for some historical periods is not very homogeneous: it is richer for the 15th century than it is for the centuries going between the 12th and 14th, for which the architectural scenario is that of a town that is expanding towards its borders, whose newly-erected edifices have not been studied at length.

4. In short, Guido Zucconi, has not been prompted by a feeling of "love" for this town to gather in the following pages a wealth of information and critical notes on the architecture of Venetian edifices, like what had occurred to Giulio Lorenzetti in 1926 with *Venice and its lagoon*. We find here none of the *pathos* which is still to be found in the latest edition of what for entire generations of visitors has been regarded as Venice's guide-book par excellence. There is no intention whatever of lea-

6.
Joseph Heintz the younger
Sea-view of the Point of the Salute, the Custom House, the Collegio Somasco *and the* Church, XVIIth century. Venice, Library of the Patriarchal Seminary.

7.
Plant of the Island of
Rialto.
L. Cicognara, A. Diedo
and G. Selva
*The Most Conspicuous
Edifices in Venice,
Measured, Illustrated
and Engraved by the
Members of the
Venetian Academy of
Fine Arts.*
Venice, 1815-20.

ding the reader through the "millenary life" of this "great peo-
ple;" far be the "dismay" expressed by the Venetian before the
art and history of "a world of its own." This new editorial under-
taking can be compared to a tool-case which has been judiciously
filled with the items best suited for setting the visitor on the prop-
er route and reading path. The brief introductions to each of the
eight chapters describe the stylistic history of the town, dwelling
briefly on the places in which it emerges most clearly, also pro-
viding a small map.

The first source of difficulties was the division of the guide-book
into chapters: a stylistic and chronological scanning process. Hence,
in its quest for the city's Byzantine origins, this book runs
through an urban context borne of the great tradition of exharchs,
by dwelling on the evolution of the Medieval storehouse dwellings. On the other hand, when dealing with the Gothic Venice,
it reverts its attention to civil architecture, seeking in the edifices the traces of Lombard workmen, without forgetting to look

in the plan of private homes and convents for the elements that may reveal it. The importance attached to the culture, the training and the experience of architects, foremen and workers is a good lead even for early Renaissance architecture, which has indeed been analytically and extensively examined in other works, but whose links with the building and decorative traditions of the late Gothic period must be enhanced in order to comprehend its troubled forms of expression (fig. 10). Where is the renewal of the Cinquecento most to be found? The changes taking place in the public works of the Arsenale, the market of Rialto and Saint Mark's Square – the places where power is produced, exchanged and exerted respectively – have been thoroughly examined by experts of Venice's urban history. However, there is no popular literature summarizing these studies, only works which, at best, confine themselves to dealing with each individ-

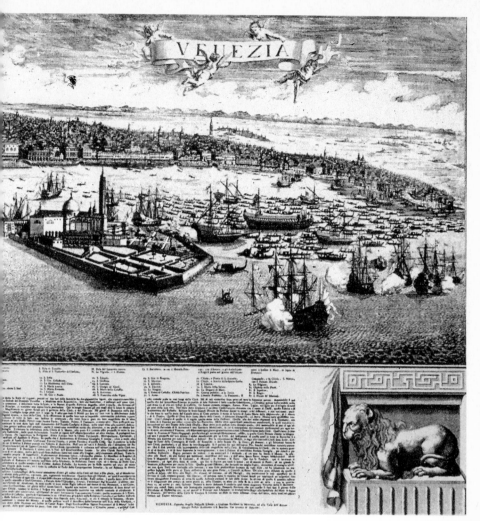

ual edifice. Even the architects of the 18th century, who share a common reference to the past (Tirali, Massari, Visentini, Temanza, Scalfarotto), and the temples of music and theatre (the church of the Pietà, the Fenice theatre) are dealt with in an effort not to forsake the philological studies carried out in other works. The simplified classicism of Napoleonic projects to be found in the edifice placed in *bocca di Piazza* (the entrance to Saint Mark's Square), in the royal gardens or in the new public facilities (such as the State Archives and the city hospital) is mentioned in a brief but detailed paragraph. The romantic myth of nostalgia and decadence, found in the buildings of great hotels, banks, insurance companies and others (that is, the places that testify to the town's modernisation), or at Lido, with its beach and holiday homes, is tackled with similar care and awareness. Nor can the competitive and the "historical" Venice which developed on the islands be for-

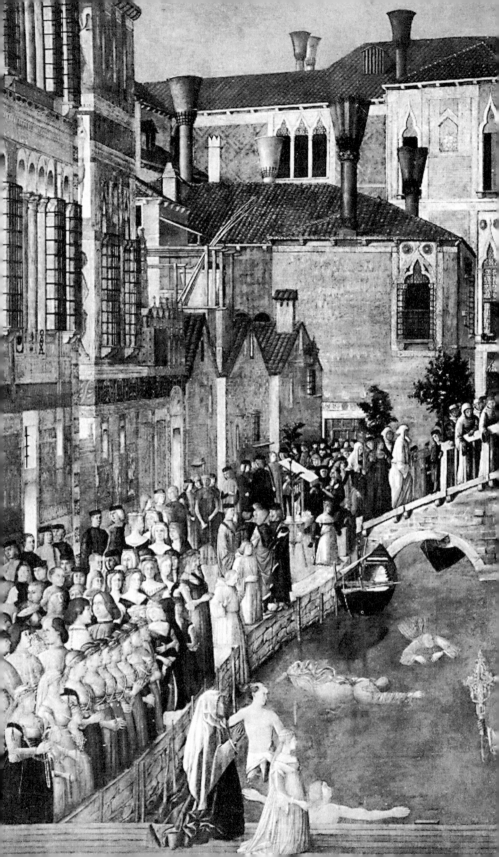

9-10.
Gentile Bellini
The Miracle of the Cross at the San Lorenzo Bridge, 1500.
Close-up view of the sea-shore, the building facing it, the small houses (to the left), and the small wooden bridge that leads direclty to the building from the canal (to the right).
Venice, Gallerie dell'Accademia.

11.
Jacopo Tintoretto
Votive Portrait of the Doge Nicolò da Ponte.
In the ground, a close-up view of the Riva degli Schiavoni.
Venice, Doge's Palace, Council Hall.

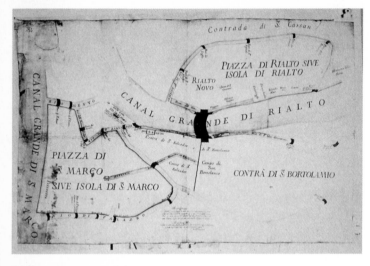

saken, that is, the harbour and the industrial centre. Lastly, come the difficulties of modern architecture, with its controversial stylistic intrusions entrapped within a highly dense building fabric (Scarpa), or rejected (Wright, Le Corbusier, Khan) or marked by a concept of a lagoon-style building tradition (Gardella). Albeit concisely, as the size of the book requires, the author does not neglect "useful information," the full address or the closest *vaporetto* stop, details which are usually provided only for mainland cities.

5. The twofold urban centrality, which is symmetrical to the umbilical cord of the Mercerie (a long street linking Rialto to Saint Mark's Square), is the global context and point of reference to which the study of Venetian edifices must be related (fig. 13). The double urban structure, on either side of the Grand Canal, the relationship existing between the main water body and the waterways in the two systems of the Saint Mark's and Rialto areas, the special relationship which developed in the lagoon between

18

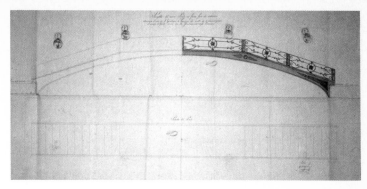

14.
The new iron bridge in
the Ghetto Nuovo,
project by engineer
Neville, 1862.
Venice, Celestia,
Municipal Archives.

its centre and the outskirts, that gradually changed between the 15th and 19th centuries, form the global urban structure which is dwelt upon at length in the stylistic and chronological routes suggested in the following pages. Even when this basic context is not explicitly mentioned, the information given implicitly makes reference to it, for indeed the author is well aware that earliest settlements in the lagoon are a reflection of it. The public works carried out at the end of the 15th century and the beginning of the 16th are noteworthy both for their size and configuration. In particular, they betray an intention which, although unvoiced, is clearly traceable: that of creating major urban routes. The two areas of Saint Mark's and Rialto in particular, as well as their surroundings, were completely transformed. Perhaps the competent authorities took advantage of the tragic events which seem to have struck Venice much too often, as well as other ancient European towns; or perhaps they simply exacerbated the need for modernisation, cleaning and clearing up of those areas which the presence of ruins and conditions of degradation had rendered indecorous. The author is also well aware of the fact that they had intended to enhance the different purposes of these two areas and their significance for the city, by eliminating some of their similarities as well as the too many mixtures of mercantile with official elements; indeed without actually referring to each individual stage, he makes implicit reference to them in his descriptions of the buildings in the areas surrounding both. It is no coincidence that their reconstruction paved the way for the building of the modern town, resorting to formal characters and to an altogether different architectural form of expression. This city planning approach constituted a binding choice for the future. Its achievement was at times entrusted to unknown overseers and anonymous foremen, and at times to famous architects. This also led to the integration into the city of new and old buildings, the creation of a new, conscious, relationship

19

between the city and the unbuilt areas of its islands, and to the remaking of the town's main routes. Indeed, the urban history of Venice has actually recorded several projects that were able not to forsake its medieval heritage and vested interests; projects, which, at the same time, did not miss the opportunity of suggesting preferential destinations.

It is very well known that the capital of the Venetian Republic was a town of trade and traders, that, for centuries, its power was based on money and political strength, that it did not draw its authority from the land and that the relevance of its financial system affected the whole of Europe. On the other hand, thinking that all of the above is to be linked to a lifestyle which developed according to patterns that were unusual for other European states would be too automatic a deduction. Indeed, anyone aware of the physical boundaries of the town and of the singular nature of its living habits cannot but realize that its urbanized fabric is the result of a community which organised itself by adapting and transforming a difficult natural site. A construction plan can therefore proceed on the basis of individual decisions and sectors, provided that the parts to which it refers be relatively clear (fig. 4). This is where Venice's "artificial style," as opposed to a natural style (on which artists and travellers dwell at length) clearly emerges: in the construction and tormentedly continuous maintenance of the network of canals, in the distribution of the various ethnic groups, in a special area like the ancient Jewish cemetery of San Nicolò – places in which the artifices that transform and embellish nature also symbolize a wisdom based on experience and a spirit of tolerance towards foreigners acquired through the city's long-standing mercantile tradition (fig. 12). There is yet another important assumption for the detailed analysis reported in the files which make up this book, that is, the frequency with which certain building materials are used in the lagoon city: the stone of Istria (for portico pillars and open galleries, for the frames of doors and windows and for some furnishings), Montello wood (for floor trusses), bricks and bent tiles from the area of Treviso and Padua (for wall surfaces and roofings). The fact that these came from the lands of the Dominion became a motivation for the exploitation of the regions belonging to Venice's sphere of influence, which otherwise lacked these materials locally, as well as an extraordinary means of linguistic unification and a formidable incentive for their continuous re-usage in various parts of the buildings (fig. 15).

Lastly, we have an extremely clear perception of a town which continuously transforms itself onto itself: all of its buildings have a centuries-old history, including the ones which in the book's files are described as belonging to a precise age or style: Renaissance churches were erected onto pre-existing Byzantine ones; palaces and dwellings were continuously remade, from the late Middle Ages to the times when Venice, like all other cities of the national state, was reached by the winds of progress – something that appears to be measurable in terms of construction standards, of the presence of hygienic and luminous dwellings, of wide streets and new iron bridges (fig. 14). Hence, in composing a picture, it is unnecessary to give a detailed emphasis of the items of the frame, if the place of each wedge within the picture is quite clear – as this attempt at utter concision seems to confirm.

21

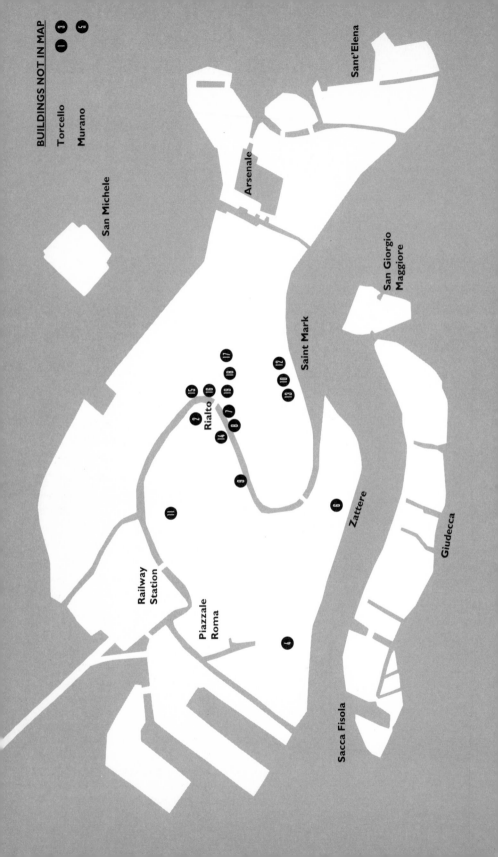

BUILDINGS NOT IN MAP

Torcello ① ③

Murano ⑤

San Michele

Railway
Station

Piazzale
Roma

Sacca Fisola

Arsenale

Sant'Elena

Rialto

Saint Mark

San Giorgio
Maggiore

Zattere

Giudecca

Medieval and Byzantine Venice

Two architectural complexes contain the preponderance of structures of historical and architectural interest; on the one hand, there is Torcello, which belongs to an early phase linked to the settlement of the outer islands, and on the other, there is Saint Mark's, the monument and symbol of a city-state that, in consolidating its institutions in a centralized area, was attaining awareness of its commercial and political strength. Both of these buildings show, in different times and forms, a clear Byzantine origin, especially deriving from that "exarchal" version that had its first centre of expansion in Ravenna, spreading naturally over the northern Adriatic region and finding its "best suited successor" in Venice, to quote an expression used by Sergio Bettini. Far less impressive are the surviving instances of civil architecture. For the most part these are parts of porticoed façades of the Veneto-Byzantine type, marked by elongated arches which, right up to the dawn of the modern age, constituted the prevailing note in the city landscape. In these remains of houses and fondaci – or storehouses, which were once a fundamental part of the existence of the city – it is possible to retrace the phases of a stylistic evolution that leads up to the beginning of the Gothic manner. In the name of an abstract notion of Veneto-Byzantine style, in the 19th century the façade of the Fondaco dei Turchi was completely reinvented.

1

Cathedral of Torcello
11th century

Actv: Torcello vaporetto stop

Founded as an episcopal seat in the 7th century, this church dedicated to Santa Maria Assunta underwent later modifications in the 9th and 11th centuries; the structure with its strongly Veneto-Byzantine flavor enjoys a remarkable state of preservation. The historical and artistic interest of this monument is enhanced by the almost surreal isolation of the site, once densely populated. An example of the continuity of late Roman culture can be seen in the basilica plan, with three aisles, punctuated by marble columns; on the interior of the main front and on the inside of the three semi-circular apses, mosaics of the school of Ravenna can be seen.

BIBLIOGRAPHY: *Bettini 1939; Forlati 1939; Lorenzoni 1983, pp. 409; Polacco 1984*

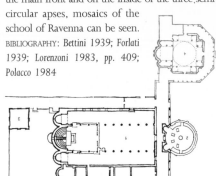

2

Church of San Giacomo at Rialto (San Giacometto)
11th century
San Polo, Campo di Rialto

Actv: San Silvestro or Rialto vaporetto stop

This is traditionally said to be the oldest church in Venice. Perhaps that is why the series of renovations carried out, especially in the 16th and 17th centuries, tended to respect the original layout. The interior is rectangular in outline; inscribed within the rectangle is a cross-shaped plan with a central dome. This model was adopted for 15th and 16th-century churches.

BIBLIOGRAPHY: *Gardani 1966; Franzoi-Di Stefano 1976, pp. 16 ff.; Calabi 1987, pp. 96 ff.*

24

3

Church of Santa Fosca at Torcello
11th century

Actv: Torcello vaporetto stop

Originally built as a martyrium adjacent to the basilica of Torcello, the church is built on a central plan. The form of a Greek cross inscribed within an octagon borrows forms typical of Byzantine architecture of the 11th century. Five of the eight outer walls are girded by a portico with stilted arches, with sculpted columns and capitals. The pentagonal apse extends along the other three sides; flanking it are semicircular apsidioles. Despite its remarkable volumetric complexity, the building appears to be a balanced and harmonious composition of an elementary geometric type.

BIBLIOGRAPHY: Bettini 1939; Forlati 1939; Vecchi 1979; Lorenzoni 1983, pp. 417 ff.

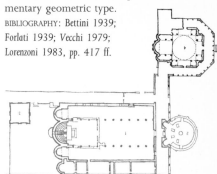

4

Church of San Nicolò dei Mendicoli
12th-16th centuries
Dorsoduro, San Nicolò

Actv: Santa Marta or San Basilio vaporetto stop

This is traditionally considered to be one of the oldest churches in Venice. The basilica layout, with three aisles set on columns, survives from the original building (7th century). Rebuilt often between the 12th and 16th centuries, it presents a bare front in brickwork, in which the 15th century portico – a feature that was once common in Venetian religious architecture – is particularly noteworthy.

BIBLIOGRAPHY: Lorenzetti 1963, pp. 551 ff.; Franzoi-Di Stefano 1976, pp. 190 ff.

5

Church of Santi Maria e Donato
11th-12th centuries (completed in 1140)
Murano, Fondamenta Giustiniani

Actv: Museo vaporetto stop

This is one of the major religious complexes founded on the islands of the lagoon during the earliest phases of settlement (7th century), and remodelled after the year 1000 on a basilical plan. The bare front elevation reflects the structure of the interior, which is split into three aisles, and divided by a tall transept. The appearance of the sides and the apses is quite well known, and this area most clearly reveals the radical restoration that was done between 1858 and 1873. During that restoration Camillo Boito decided to rebuild the church's outer shell, using brick; the exterior featured concentric brick niches which, toward the end, are transformed into a double order of small arches set on slender paired columns.

BIBLIOGRAPHY: Lorenzetti 1963, p. 817; Fontana 1981

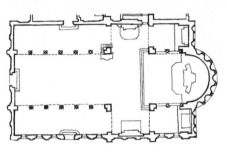

6

Church of Sant'Agnese
12th-13th centuries
Dorsoduro, Rio Terrà Alboretti

Actv: Zattere vaporetto stop

This church, which has been deconsecrated, has undergone a great deal of renovation and remodelling; the last episode of renovation (1939) was intended to restore to the church the features of a typical Veneto-Byzantine building; despite all this renovation, one can clearly detect the features of a pure basilica, with three aisles and no transept, much more than in other buildings in Venice.

BIBLIOGRAPHY: Lorenzetti 1963, pp. 522 ff.; Franzoi-Di Stefano 1976, pp. 213 ff.

7
Ca' Loredan
12th century
San Marco 4137, Riva del Carbon
Actv: Rialto vaporetto stop

This has housed City Hall since 1868; although it has undergone a great deal of renovation (and two floors have been added), it still preserves the original capitals, columns, and paterae in the lower loggia and in the upper arcades which covers the entire façade. About this polyforate window, Sergio Bettini spoke of a "façade that is entirely devoured by the polyforate window."

BIBLIOGRAPHY: Bettini 1978, p. 101; Maretto 1986, pp. 76 ff.

8
Ca' Farsetti
12th century
San Marco 4136, Riva del Carbon
Actv: Rialto vaporetto stop

This building now houses city offices, and is well known as a sister palazzo to Ca' Loredan. The two buildings face the Grand Canal, and together they constitute a sort of Veneto-Byzantine continuum; more heavily renovated than Ca' Loredan, Ca' Farsetti presents a remarkable sequence of slender paired columns, which support the stilted arches.

BIBLIOGRAPHY: Lorenzetti 1963, pp. 489 ff.; Zorzi-Marton 1989, pp. 54 ff.

9
Ca' Donà della Madonetta
12th-13th centuries
San Polo 1429/b, Calle del Traghetto
Actv: San Silvestro vaporetto stop

Together with the adjacent Casa Donà, this building looks out over the Grand Canal with a long polyforate window, which Edoardo Arslan has identified as typical of the first phase of Veneto-Byzantine residential architecture. There are semicircular arches, set on extremely ornate capitals.

BIBLIOGRAPHY: Arslan 1970, p. 21; Maretto 1986 pp. 86 ff.

10

Saint Mark's Cathedral
9th century (rebuilt in the 11th century);
façades from the 12th to 16th centuries
Saint Mark's Square

Actv: San Marco or San Zaccaria vaporetto stop

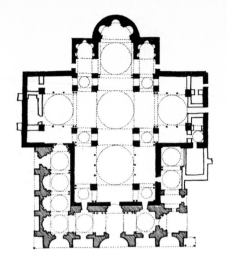

The first building was erected by the Partecipa-zio family, in 829-832, and it was to serve two purposes: to house the relics of Saint Mark the Evangelist, and as a palatine chapel for the nearby Doge's palace (the character and function of city temple were to persist over time; it became an episcopal church only in 1807). The structure was modelled after the 6th century Church of the Apostles in Constantinople. The plan involved a Greek cross inscribed in a square; at the center,

standing above the four arms of the cross shape, was a series of large domes. An instance of "antiquarian eclecticism," that had been develop-ed with an eye to some of the most modern examples of the times, both of Romanesque and of Greek derivation. Despite the evident and spectacular presence of the vast mosaics and the domes with their golden background, Byzan-tine art here represented a substrate, upon which a number of different references were gradually accumulating, and merging in a great stylistic synthesis. Even more than in the interior, this aspect can be seen in the original fronts added to the building between the 12th and 15th centu-ries. On three sides of the basilica, a sort of gal-lery overlooks the square, with a double order of arches and niches, divided by a terrace with a baluster, surmounted by Gothic pinnacles.

BIBLIOGRAPHY: Bettini 1946; Mariacher-Pignatti 1950; Demus 1960; Krautheimer 1986, pp. 440 ff.

11
Church of San Giacomo dell'Orio
12th-13th centuries
Santa Croce, Campo San Giacomo dell'Orio
Actv: Riva di Biasio or San Stae vaporetto stop

Perhaps this church was founded in the 11th century, but the current building dates from the 13th century, and underwent successive alterations. The basilical plan was modified by the insertion of a transept, in line with a Latin cross plan. Also worthy of mention are the ship's-keel wooden ceiling (14th century) and the Veneto-Byzantine bell tower (12th century).
BIBLIOGRAPHY: Lorenzetti 1963, pp. 604 ff.; Franzoi-Di Stefano 1976, pp. 69 ff.

12
Cloister of Sant'Apollonia
12th-13th centuries
Castello 4312, ponte della Canonica
Actv: San Zaccaria vaporetto stop

This is the only example of a 13th-century cloister; it once belonged to the congregation of the Primiceri of Saint Mark's. The sequence of small semicircular arches is supported by slender columns, both single and paired. The 15th-century portal leads to the Scuola of the Linaroli, which had originally been dedicated to Saint Apollonia. The Jesurum company now occupies the building.
BIBLIOGRAPHY: Lorenzetti 1963, pp. 320 ff.; Zorzi-Marton 1989, pp. 60 ff.

13
Albergo del Selvadego
13th century
San Marco, Calle dell'Ascensione
Actv: San Marco vaporetto stop

The thorough-going restoration executed by F. Forlati (1926) brought to light typical features of Veneto-Byzantine architecture, emphasized and highlighted by the dark brick façade. On the upper floor is a continuous roofed loggia, on the intermediate floor is a series of elongated windows with stilted arches. In the 19th century, this building belonged to the painter Ippolito Caffi.
BIBLIOGRAPHY: Lorenzetti 1963, p. 462

14

Ca' Barzizza
12th-13th century
San Polo 1172-73, Campiello Barzizza
Actv: San Silvestro vaporetto stop

In this building overlooking the Grand Canal, the most interesting features are the polyforate window on the main floor and the decorated portal on the ground floor; the cusped arches with extrados are linked, in the opinion of Arslan, to the second phase of Veneto-Byzantine civil architecture.

BIBLIOGRAPHY: *Arslan 1963, p. 462*

15

Ca' da Mosto
13th century
Cannaregio 5628, Corte del Leon Bianco
Actv: Ca' d'Oro vaporetto stop

For many years, this was the site of the Albergo del Leon Bianco (hence the name of the square) and it may be the best known of all the Veneto-Byzantine buildings that look out over the Grand Canal. Worthy of note is the regular sequence of cusped arches that surmount the polyforate window on the main floor; these arches seem to counterbalance the irregularity of the lower loggia, originally built as a storehouse.

BIBLIOGRAPHY: *Arslan 1970, p. 25; Zorzi-Marton 1989*, pp. 64 ff.

16

Ca' Lioni
13th century
Cannaregio, Campiello del Remer
Actv: Ca' d'Oro or Rialto vaporetto stop

One can still detect the original structure of a *casa da stazio con magazzeni* (warehouse with docks), arranged around a courtyard; the external stairway leads to the residential area, set above the "vaults," which were used as a storehouse. The ogee arches reveal the clear influence of Eastern models.

BIBLIOGRAPHY: *Lorenzetti 1963, p. 395; Concina 1989*, p. 42

17

Palazzo Vitturi

13th century

Cannaregio 5246, Campo Santa Maria Formosa

Actv: Rialto or San Zaccaria vaporetto stop

Here, as in Palazzo Priuli near San Stae, and in other buildings from the same period, the main façade shows stylistic features typical of the late-13th-century transition. Influenced by Eastern and Gothic motifs, even the intrados of the arch of the polyforate window is cusped. John Ruskin described this as belonging to the final phase of mature Gothic style.

BIBLIOGRAPHY: *Arslan 1970, p. 31*

18

Palazzetto at San Lio

13th century

Castello 5691-5705, Salizzada San Lio

Actv: Rialto vaporetto stop

This is not an example of a large merchant's home based on the traditional three-part scheme. To emphasize the widespread diffusion of Byzantine models, here the handsome polyforate window and doors are framed by great stone piers and carved lintels. Thus such a characteristic Venetian fashion was also fitting to an ordinary building pattern.

BIBLIOGRAPHY: *Trincanato 1948, pp. 127 ff.*

19

Palazzo Moro

13th century

San Marco 5309-10, Campo San Bartolomeo

Actv: Rialto vaporetto stop

The double sequence of arched windows allows us to compare two phases of stylistic development: the 15th-century polyforate window on the main floor, in fact, has semicircular arches, while the polyforate window on the upper floor has cusped arches, and seems to foreshadow the 14th-century shapes. Of some note is the carved stone balustrade.

BIBLIOGRAPHY: *Arslan 1970, p. 31*

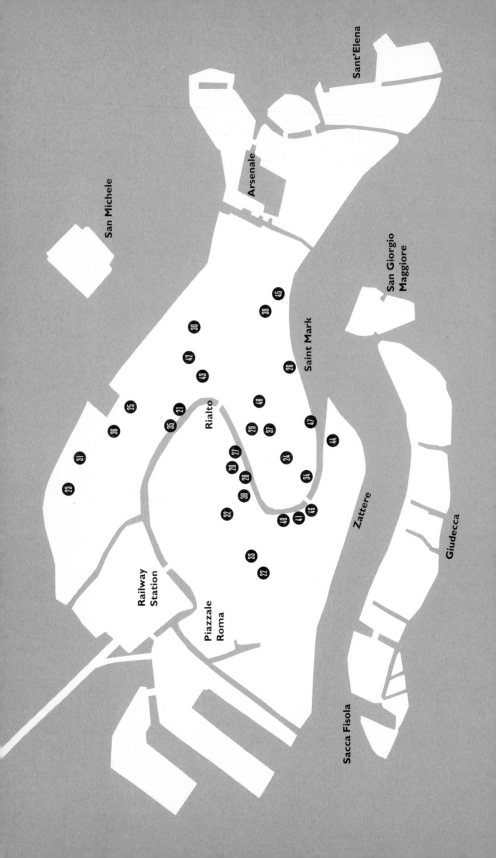

Gothic and Late-Gothic Venice

It seems that a specific character of Venetian Gothic developed in all the areas connected with architecture. At first in the building of the Doge's Palace, and then in the chief façade of Ca' d'Oro, a style was codified that found its best known expression in the so-called trefoil window. This is to say the geometric interweaving of curved and inflected lines that seems to challenge – in arches, rose-windows, and volutes – the static properties of stone and the technical skills of the craftsmen, just emerging from centuries of anonymity: names like Raverti, Bon, and Delle Masegne, members of dynasties of builders, often originally from Lombardy. With the polyforate window with inflected arches, set at the centre of the façade, the Venetian palazzo crystallized its structure into a form that emphasized its three-part layout. In the centre was the elongated hall (pòrtego), arranged perpendicular to the main elevation; along both sides are series of smaller rooms, connected one to another (torreselle). Religious architecture, too, attained forms of stylistic and structure codification: in the great examples of convent architecture, and especially in the two closely linked buildings of San Zanipolo and Frari, late Venetian Gothic showed a powerful capacity for expression, and an ability to find local versions of the distinctive features of an international style.

20

Palazzo Soranzo at San Polo
14th-15th centuries
San Polo 2170-71, Campo San Polo
Actv: San Silvestro or San Tomà vaporetto stop

The sequence of façades clearly reiterates the terms of a stylistic transition from 14th-century forms and late-Gothic models. The two entry portals, in medieval style, are counterbalanced by the polyforate windows on the upper floor. At number 2169 we find the part that was built in thorough conformity with 15th-century canons.
BIBLIOGRAPHY: *Maretto 1986, p. 137; Zorzi-Marton 1989, pp. 126 ff.*

21

Palazzo Sagredo at Santa Sofia
14th century
Cannaregio 4199, Strada Nuova
Actv: Ca' d'Oro vaporetto stop

In the façade on the Grand Canal and in the façade overlooking Campo Santa Sofia, we can still clearly see the 14th-century layout. The row of windows of Byzantine origin is here transformed into a series of ogee and trefoil arches which are clear forerunners of the late-Gothic polyforate window. The interiors were renovated during the 18th century.
BIBLIOGRAPHY: *Arslan 1970, pp. 134 ff.; Zorzi-Marton 1989 pp. 118 ff.*

22

Palazzo Arian Cicogna near the Carmini
14th century
Dorsoduro 2376, Fondamenta Briati
Actv: Ca' Rezzonico or San Basilio vaporetto stop

In the hexaforate window of the main façade we see, for the first time in Venetian Gothic architecture, the trefoil window that will attain its greatest triumph in the Doge's Palace. Above the gothic vaults is an extremely fine ornamental motif in stone, clearly derived from Eastern models.
BIBLIOGRAPHY: *Arslan 1970, pp. 80 ff.; Zorzi-Marton 1989, pp. 122 ff.*

23

Church of Sant'Alvise

14th century (completed in 1388)
Cannaregio 3282, Campo Sant'Alvise

Actv: Sant'Alvise vaporetto stop

Despite the later renovations, this church presents itself as an example of Gothic convent architecture of the 14th century. The bare brick façade (with oculi and a central portal) corresponds on the interior to a single aisle and a low ceiling. Above the entryway is one of the first examples of hanging choir (*barco*), reserved for nuns.

BIBLIOGRAPHY: *Lorenzetti 1963*, p. 409; *Franzoi-Di Stefano 1976*, pp. 129 ff.

24

Church of Santo Stefano

14th century
San Marco 3825, Campo Santo Stefano

Actv: Sant'Angelo or Accademia or San Samuele vaporetto stop

Founded by the Eremitani in the 13th century, this church was later rebuilt to the standards of a simplified Gothic. There are three aisles and no transept, and simple wooden columns support the wooden roof, fashioned in the shape of a ship's hull. Among the 14th-century decorations, of particular interest is the entry portal, built by Bartolomeo Bon.

BIBLIOGRAPHY: *Lorenzetti 1963*, p. 502 ff.; *Franzoi-Di Stefano 1976*, pp. 333 ff.

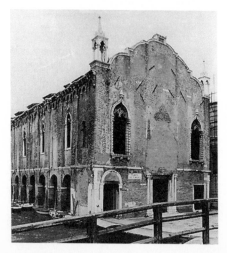

25

Scuola Vecchia della Misericordia

14th-15th centuries .
Cannaregio, Campo dell'Abbazia

Actv: San Marcuola or Ca' d'Oro vaporetto stop

The origin of this building was in the 14th century, when the Great Guild whose name it bears was founded. The actual structure dates from the 15th century, and is largely attributed to the school of the Bon family. The front has a curved crown that connects a series of symmetrical features – one of the side portals leads to a public passage (*sottoportico*), built in 1508.

BIBLIOGRAPHY: *Howard 1975*, pp. 98 ff.

26

Doge's Palace

14th-15th centuries (completed in 1438)
Saint Mark's Square

Actv: San Marco or San Zaccaria vaporetto stop

Nothing now survives of the original Byzantine building, founded by the Partecipazio family in the 9th century. The structure now standing was the product of reconstruction that began in the late 13th century on the hall of the Maggior Consiglio, and its subsequent expansion. After 1340, on the side overlooking the wharf, the distinctive façade split up horizontally into three strips began to take shape. The upper layer was the *piano* (corresponding to the hall), in the middle was the loggia with ogee arch with inflection in the crown carved in the form of a four-lobed leaf, and at the bottom was a portico supported by stout columns directly on the ground and by a series of ogee arches. Tradition has it that the stone craftman Filippo Calendario was responsible for the stylistic and structural approach, which was destined to become not only the symbol of Gothic Venice, but also a concrete model for civil architecture. This is especially true of the central arcade of the façade, where the motif of geometric interweaving,

Arabic and Islamic in origin, melded with the local tradition (this hybrid nature, linked to a remarkable craftsmanship in its execution, that later so intrigued John Ruskin and the other Romantic critics). Beginning in 1424, under Doge Francesco Foscari, and in conformity with the established forms, the side facing the *piazzetta* was completed. At the end of the pre-Renaissance phase, the Porta della Carta (1442) serves to emphasize the late Gothic character carved into the façades. From now on, the attention of architects, stonecarvers, and decorators was to focus on the eastern wing, the courtyard, and the interiors (see entry no. 68).

BIBLIOGRAPHY: *Mariacher 1950; Trincanato 1970; Bettini 1978, pp. 59 ff.*

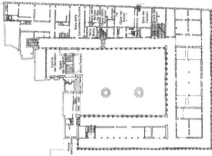

27

Palazzo Bernardo near Campo San Polo
15th century
San Polo 2195, Calle del Scaleter
Actv: San Silvestro or San Tomà vaporetto stop
A typical example of 15th-century building style, based on a layout that balanced the inner courtyard with the façade on the Grand Canal. Here the polyforate window appears to have been heavily influenced by the Doge's Palace: we find the quadrifoil tracery interwoven with the large windows with inflected arches.
BIBLIOGRAPHY: *Arslan 1970, p. 146; Maretto 1986, p. 244*

28

Palazzo Pisani Moretta
15th century
San Polo 2766
Actv: San Tomà vaporetto stop
Another example of late-Gothic architecture overlooking the Grand Canal. Of particular importance are the tracery windows that overlook the canal and which, here too, are influenced by the Doge's Palace model. The interior offers a complete example of 18th-century furnishings and decorations.
BIBLIOGRAPHY: *Maretto 1986, p. 150*

29

Palazzo Pesaro degli Orfei
15th century
San Marco 3858, Campo San Beneto
Actv: Sant'Angelo vaporetto stop
One of the largest palazzi in Venice, this building features, on three sides, a remarkable series of late-Gothic façades; in terms of stylistic integrity and consistency, this is certainly one of the most important examples of this sort. It was once the home of the artist Mariano Fortuny, and it now houses the offices of the foundation that bears his name.
BIBLIOGRAPHY: *Arslan 1970, pp. 253 ff.; Zorzi-Marton 1989, pp. 170 ff.*

30

Church of the Santi Giovanni e Paolo (or San Zanipolo)

14th-15th centuries (completed in 1430)
Castello, Campo dei Santi Giovanni e Paolo

Actv: Fondamente Nuove or Ospedale vaporetto stop

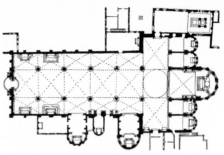

Of 13th-century origins, but later rebuilt, this great Dominican church constitutes the most complete example of Gothic religious architecture in the city. Pantheon of the Republic of Venice, this church, like the Church of the Frari, built around the same time, has a Latin-cross plan, with three aisles and a transept. Polygonal

apses terminate the arms of a plan that, especially on the interior, appears quite simplified in comparison with the canons of gothic art; the ogee arches and the cross-vault ceilings are supported by large stone pillars, linked together by wooden chains (all features that we find again in the Church of the Frari).

BIBLIOGRAPHY: Caccin 1964; Zava Boccazzi 1965; Franzoi-Di Stefano 1976, pp. 424 ff.

31

Church of the Madonna dell'Orto

14th-15th centuries
Cannaregio, Campo Madonna dell'Orto

Actv: Madonna dell'Orto vaporetto stop

This can be considered, more or less, a third case in the group of the churches of the Frari and San Zanipolo. We find here, in a smaller size and in greatly simplified form, the features that typify the religious architecture of the 14th and 15th centuries (the big brick structure body, the three-part composition of the façade and the plan).

BIBLIOGRAPHY: Lorenzetti 1963, pp. 403 ff.; Franzoi-Di Stefano 1976, pp. 132 ff.

32

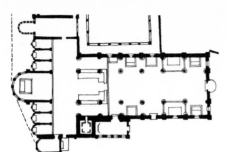

Church of Santa Maria Gloriosa dei Frari
14th-15th centuries (completed in 1433)
San Polo, Campo dei Frari
Actv: San Tomà vaporetto stop

Founded in the 13th century, and later rebuilt, this Franciscan church appears now as a large building made entirely of brick. The three-part façade has a rose-window and a mixed-style crown; the façade is marked by massive pilasters that appear along the sides as well. Inside and out, in terms of style and layout, the building shows simplified Gothic features, remarkably

similar to those found in San Zanipolo, built at the same time (and, like San Zanipolo, it constitutes a pantheon of the glories of Venice). In the huge former convent, where the first cloister of clearly 17th-century design is of particular note, the State Archives are located.

BIBLIOGRAPHY: *Fogolari 1931; Sartori 1949; Franzoi-Di Stefano 1976, pp. 33 ff.*

33

Church of the Carmini
13th-14th century (completed in 1348), renovated in the 16th century
Dorsoduro, Campo dei Carmini
Actv: Ca' Rezzonico or San Basilio vaporetto stop

A large Gothic building laid out on a basilical plan; like the church of the Madonna dell'Orto, it lacks a transept. Both the polygonal apse and the façade with its three curved pediments belong to the 16th-century phase, while the 14th-century cloister now belongs to the Istituto d'Arte (street address number 3116/a).

BIBLIOGRAPHY: *Niero 1965; Franzoi-Di Stefano 1976, pp. 177 ff.*

34

Palazzo Barbaro near Santo Stefano
15th century
San Marco 2840, Fondamenta Barbaro

Actv: Accademia or Santa Maria del Giglio vaporetto stop

Like the adjacent Palazzo Cavalli Franchetti (rebuilt in the 19th century; see entry no. 213), the building offers, in the elevation overlooking the Grand Canal, an example of gothic architecture of the early 15th century, which became common in Venice on the model of the Doge's Palace.

BIBLIOGRAPHY: *Arslan 1970, p. 235; Zorzi-Marton 1989, pp. 222 ff.*

35

Ca' d'Oro
1421-1443
Cannaregio 3933, Calle della Ca' d'Oro

Actv: Ca' d'Oro vaporetto stop

With its polychrome and inlaid marble, its gilt decorations (which survive only in the name), the façade on the Grand Canal appears as a spectacular, almost virtuoso expression of the so-called Flamboyant Gothic. Craftsmen who had previously worked on the Doge's Palace worked on this palazzo, built for Marino Contarini; the art of stone tracery in this case attained remarkable heights of technical skill and decorative imagination. The decorative array was used here to adorn the traditional structure of a merchant's home (note the loggia on the front and the inner courtyard). Since 1927, the palazzo has housed the art collection of the Galleria Franchetti.

BIBLIOGRAPHY: *Lorenzetti 1963, pp. 423, 637 ff.; Arslan 1970, pp. 225 ff.*

36

Palazzo Mastelli near the Misericordia
15th century
Cannaregio 3381, Campo dei Mori
Actv: Madonna dell'Orto vaporetto stop

This building is called "del Cammello" because of the high-relief, to the right of the balcony, that seems to depict the owners, originally from the Levant. Both motifs borrowed from Ca' d'Oro and reminiscences of Eastern flavour must have influenced the gothic loggia at the center of the façade.

BIBLIOGRAPHY: Lorenzetti 1963, p. 403; Zorzi-Marton 1989, pp. 218 ff.

37

Palazzo Duodo at Sant'Angelo
15th century
San Marco 3584, Campo Sant'Angelo
Actv: Sant'Angelo vaporetto stop

A handsome example of a late-Gothic palazzetto, this belongs to that group of civic buildings that does not seem to have been influenced by the models of the early 15th century. It has no tracery, it features a series of polyforate windows with inflected arches set within a marble field. Facing it is Palazzo Gritti (street address number 3832), which mirrors it in a number of aspects.

BIBLIOGRAPHY: Lorenzetti 1963, p. 507

38

Palazzo Centani near San Tomà
15th century
San Polo 2794, Calle dei Nomboli
Actv: San Tomà vaporetto stop

In many features of the façade, this building is similar to Palazzo Duodo; on the interior, there is a handsome courtyard with an external two-ramp staircase. In 1707, the playwright Carlo Goldoni was born here; it was made into a museum in 1952, and belongs to the Institute for Theater Studies.

BIBLIOGRAPHY: Lorenzetti 1963, p. 575; Zorzi-Marton 1989, pp. 206 ff.

39

Palazzo Priuli near San Severo
15th century
Castello 4979, Rio di San Severo and
Rio di San Provolo
Actv: San Zaccaria vaporetto stop

Alongside many features typical of a late-Gothic layout, simplified to a certain extent, the façade facing the Rio (which was once covered with frescoes by Palma the Elder) presents a singular corner motif with a biforate window and a balcony; in his book, *The Stones of Venice* (1853), John Ruskin analyzes it and describes it as typical of Venetian art.

BIBLIOGRAPHY: *Lorenzetti 1963*, p. 320

40

Ca' Foscari
15th century (begun in 1452)
Dorsoduro 3246, Calle Foscari
Actv: San Tomà or Ca' Rezzonico vaporetto stop

With the adjacent Palazzo Giustinian, comprising two twin buildings, Ca' Foscari constitutes a single and homogeneous architectural continuum of late-Gothic flavour; the succession of façades that overlook the Grand Canal appears to be the definitive affirmation of the building type with superimposed polyforate windows (in the lower level, there is a series of trilobed ogees, in the upper levels are the features typically found in Venetian tracery, which appeared previously in the Doge's Palace and the Ca' d'Oro). Above the Gothic arcades there is a marble band with winged cherubs and other elements that hold up shields, a clear foreshadowing of the onset of the Renaissance. Ever since 1867, the building has housed the University, which takes its name from the palazzo.

BIBLIOGRAPHY: *Lorenzetti 1963*, pp. 624 ff.; *Zorzi-Marton 1989*, pp. 164 ff.

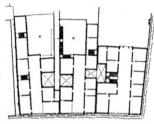

41

Palazzo Loredan dell'Ambasciatore

second half of the 15th century
Dorsoduro 1262/a, Ramo dell'Ambasciator

Actv: Ca' Rezzonico or Accademia vaporetto stop

This building, formerly the Austrian Embassy, shows – on a reduced scale – the same stylistic components found in Ca' Foscari, built at the same time. In the elevation overlooking the Grand Canal, in fact, we find a marble band with proto-Renaissance features, alongside the late-Gothic polyforate windows.

BIBLIOGRAPHY: *Lorenzetti 1963, pp. 622; Lieberman 1982, plate 13*

42

Palazzo van Axel

1473-1479
Cannaregio 6099, Fondamenta Sanudo

Actv: Rialto or Ospedale vaporetto stop

One of the most important examples of late-Gothic architecture, as we can see from the two façades with large quadriforate windows; worthy of mention are the two interior courtyards, with their open staircases. The entry portal, together with the picture of the nearby Rio della Panada, offers one of the most celebrated views of Venice.

BIBLIOGRAPHY: *Arslan 1970, pp. 252 ff.; Zorzi-Marton 1989, pp. 212 ff.*

43

Palazzo Bragadin Carabba at Santa Marina

15th century
Cannaregio 6050, Rio di San Lio

Actv: Rialto vaporetto stop

Facing the main entry (with its handsome 16th-century portal) is the façade overlooking the Rio dei Miracoli; here, alongside the typical features of the late-Gothic repertory (inflected arches framed on a field of marble) we find new decorative concepts, such as the small carved heads, which hint at the coming Renaissance.

BIBLIOGRAPHY: *Lorenzetti 1963, p. 358*

44

Former Church of San Gregorio
15th century
Dorsoduro, Campo dell'Abbazia

Actv: Salute vaporetto stop

This was part of a Benedictine abbey in the 9th century (the 14th-century cloister is now part of the private building at number 172). The three-part elevation – with rose window – overlooks the Campo, while the polygonal apse built in conformity with the model of the church of the Carità overlooks the Rio della Salute; it features tall polyforate windows.

BIBLIOGRAPHY: *Lorenzetti 1963, pp. 535 ff.; Franzoi-Di Stefano 1976, pp. 234 ff.*

45

Church of San Giovanni in Bragora
15th century
Castello, Campo Bandiera e Moro

Actv: San Zaccaria vaporetto stop

Rebuilt a number of times since the 8th century, this church preserves a façade typical of the latest Venetian Gothic, with a large central arch and curved side profiles of the top of the façade (a motif that was later developed by Codussi in his elevations). On the interior, we can clearly see the stylistic gap between the Gothic building (completed in 1479) and the presbytery, built in proto-Renaissance forms after 1490.

BIBLIOGRAPHY: *Lorenzetti 1963, pp. 295 ff.; Franzoi-Di Stefano 1976, pp. 491 ff.*

46

Former Church of the Carità
15th century (completed by Bartolomeo Bon in 1441-1452)
Dorsoduro 1049-50, Campo della Carità

Actv: Accademia vaporetto stop

Along with the Scuola and the former convent, this building forms part of the complex of the Academy of Fine Arts (see entry no. 194). The brick exterior with a triple-cusped façade and the side topped by a cornice marked by small hanging arches survives; alongside it is the 14th-century entry to the Scuola, an ogee shape, with niches and tabernacles.

BIBLIOGRAPHY: *Lorenzetti 1963, pp. 650 ff.; Franzoi-Di Stefano 1976, pp. 216 ff.*

47

Palazzetto Contarini Fasan
15th century (completed in 1475)
San Marco 2307, Campiello Contarini
Actv: San Marco vaporetto stop

An elaborate example of Flamboyant Gothic, this building is also called the House of Desdemona in obedience to a long-lived romantic legend; its limited size corresponds to the area occupied by a chopped-off tower that was used, during the Middle Ages, to hold a chain that served to close off the Grand Canal.
BIBLIOGRAPHY: Lorenzetti 1963, p. 617

48

Palazzo Contarini del Bovolo
15th century (completed in 1499)
San Marco 4299, Calle della Vida
Actv: Sant'Angelo or Rialto vaporetto stop

If the front overlooking the Rio constitutes just one more of many examples of late-Gothic architecture, the façade in the rear presents a number of original features – a spiral staircase, set inside a round tower, is joined to a loggia with five superimposed orders. The incidence of the stairway is punctuated by arches that make the union of the two structures even more difficult. This structure, which does not follow the more rigid stylistic rules, was the work of craftsman Giovanni Candi. The building, at any rate, made such an impression on the populace that the Venetian term *bovolo*, meaning "snail" (*scala a chiocciola* means "spiral staircase" in Italian) not only came to be applied to the house, but to the family itself. Inside, where the offices for the Legge Speciale (Venice conservation municipal agency) are now situated, there is a collection of 17th- and 18th-century paintings, now owned by the city.
BIBLIOGRAPHY: Lieberman 1982, plate 56; McAndrew 1983, p. 30

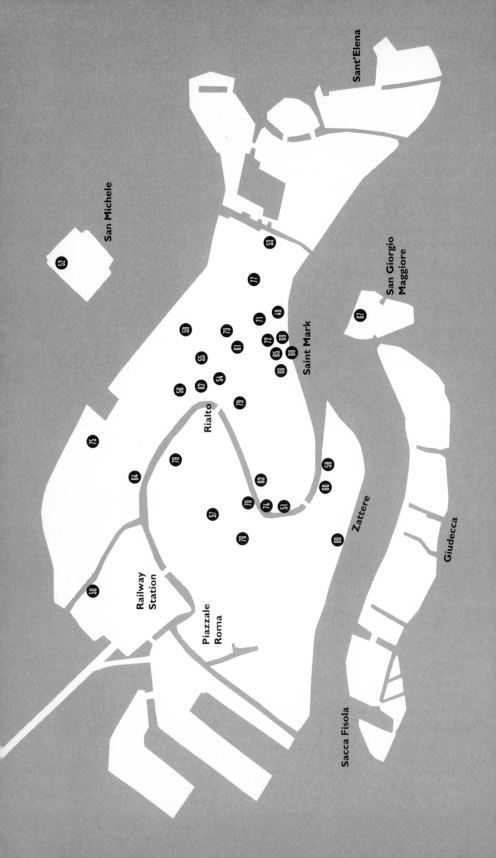

San Michele

Sant'Elena

San Giorgio
Maggiore

Saint Mark

Rialto

Zattere

Giudecca

Railway
Station

Piazzale
Roma

Sacca Fisola

50
52
53
54
55
56
57
58
59
60
61
62
63
64
65
66
67
68
69
70
71
72
73
74
75
76
77
78
79
80
81

Early Renaissance Venice

Buildings from the latter half of the 15th century, too, can be attributed to stonecutters and craftsmen who, for the most part came from those same Lombard valleys that had recently fallen under Venetian domination. Names like Bon, Lombardo, and even Codussi are inseparably linked to a tradition of building and decoration that, even at the end of the 15th century, found its expression in late-Gothic forms. This sort of language apparently coexisted with the first manifestations of a new type of architecture that was transmitted through the acolytes of Humanism, or else through direct contact in the construction yards for the new Basilica del Santo in Padua. The Gothic tracery in the façade of Ca' Foscari dates from a few years after the completion of the Porta dell'Arsenale (1460), the first instance of Renaissance art. Deriving from the techniques employed by the Proti of Lombard origin, the widespread use of polychrome marble and the elevated skill in the art of inlay together provide a certain homogeneity to works of architecture that belong to the same period that are usually considered to be at stylistic extremes: the churches of the Frari and San Zaccaria, Ca' d'Oro, and Palazzo Dario. For some time thereafter, local tradition was to serve as a filter for the new architectural models, which elsewhere in Italy reigned uncontested by the end of the 15th century; with a view to indicating that this was a phase of transition, critics therefore speak of Venetian art of the early Renaissance.

49

Church of San Zaccaria
1444-1500
Antonio Gambello and Mauro Codussi
Castello, Campo San Zaccaria
Actv: San Zaccaria vaporetto stop

Founded in the 9th century, this church was for many years under the protection of the Doges, and it served them as a sort of Pantheon. Indicator of a remarkably rapid architectural transition, the current, grandiose structure is the product of two different projects. The first employed late-Gothic forms and was completed prior to 1480, the second relied upon proto-Renaissance models. The first church, designed by Gambello, can be seen best in the San Tarasio Chapel (originally the apse), in the high basement of the façade, and in general in the tendency toward the vertical. Over all this Codussi overlaid a series of orders notable for their width, crowned by curvilinear motifs. On the interior, the Renaissance columns stand on octagonal plinths, conceived as bases for Gothic pillars.

BIBLIOGRAPHY: *Puppi-Olivato 1977*, pp. 50, 190 ff.; *McAndrew 1983*, pp. 39, 257 ff.

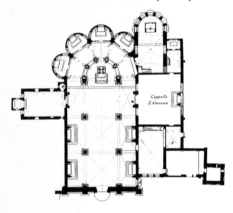

50

Church of San Giobbe
1450-1493
Antonio Gambello and Pietro Lombardo
Cannaregio, Campo San Giobbe
Actv: Tre Archi vaporetto stop

Begun under the direction of Gambello in ogee arched forms, construction went on under Pietro Lombardo with the use of early-Renaissance models. Unlike the adjacent convent, the church thus takes on the appearance of a building of the transition, particularly evident in the contrast between the nave and the presbytery, between the Lombardesque portal and the brick façade.

BIBLIOGRAPHY: *Lorenzetti 1963*, pp. 446 ff.; *McAndrew 1983*, pp. 137 ff.

51

Ca' del Duca
1461-1465
San Marco 3052, Corte del Duca
Actv: San Samuele vaporetto stop

Of the giant building intended for Francesco Sforza, Duke of Milan, only the rusticated base was completed, made with diamond-shaped blocks and with corner columns. These features, visible from the Grand Canal, were part of a huge design attributed to Filarete.

BIBLIOGRAPHY: Lieberman 1982, plate 57; McAndrew 1983, pp. 28 ff.

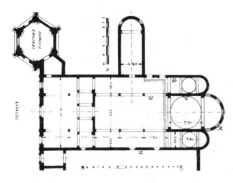

52

Church of San Michele in Isola
1469-1478
Mauro Codussi
Island of San Michele
Actv: Cimitero vaporetto stop

With its bright structure made of Istrian stone, this building was the prototype of Codussi's church design, which later spread throughout Venice and her dominions. This is especially true of the tripartite façade, with its semicircular

pediment, the central oculus, and the curvilinear buttresses. The interior appears as a re-elaboration of the three-aisled convent model; the vestibule is separated from the body of the church by the *barco*, a projecting choir intended for the monks. Alongside the façade, the hexagonal volume of the Emiliani Chapel, stands out. It was erected by Guglielmo Bergamasco around 1530; on the opposite side stands the 15th-century cloister that leads to the city cemetery, which dates from the 19th century (see entry no. 214).

BIBLIOGRAPHY: Puppi-Olivato 1977, pp. 177 ff.; McAndrew 1983, pp. 231 ff.

53
Porta Magna of the Arsenale
1460

Castello, Campo dell'Arsenale

Actv: Arsenale vaporetto stop

The triumphal arch was built under the dogeship of Pasquale Malipiero, after the Arch of the Sergi in Pola; this is the first piece of architecture in the city to be a complete expression of the new classical language. The construction of this *porta* (gate) came in the wake of a major fortification project undertaken after 1457, in response to the threat of Turk expansion, and intensified after the fall of Constantinople; a new and decisive impulse was given to this

construction after 1473, when almost twenty acres of lagoon was incorporated and turned over to the construction of a wet dock for eighty galleys, known as the Arsenal Novissimo.

BIBLIOGRAPHY: *Concina* 1984/b, pp. 51 ff., 71 ff.

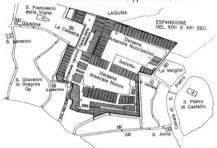

54
Gussoni Chapel in the Church of San Lio
circa 1480

Pietro and Tullio Lombardo

Castello, Campo San Lio

Actv: Rialto vaporetto stop

"Antiquarian" in style was the chapel built by the Lombardos, immediately following their work on the construction of the Basilica del Santo, where they first came into contact with the new artistic culture. During the same years, in the nearby Rio della Fava (street address number 5527), work was underway on the façade of the family palazzo, conceived with similar style and intent.

BIBLIOGRAPHY: *Lorenzetti* 1963, pp. 327 ff.; *McAndrew* 1983, p. 51

55

Church of Santa Maria dei Miracoli
1481-1494
Pietro Lombardo
Cannaregio, Campo dei Miracoli
Actv: Rialto vaporetto stop

The Lombardos designed this church with simple forms around a miracle-working image of the Virgin, setting a domed cylinder (presbytery) alongside a rectangular structure covered by barrel vaults (hall for the faithful). The polychrome marble serves as an exquisite decorative accompaniment to the difficult encounter between volumes of dissimilar shape. Actually, both in the exterior and interior faces, the stone linings were selected, cut, set, and inlaid with a remarkable level of skill and imagination. Perhaps it was with a mind to this aspect that several observers, perhaps swept away by their own enthusiasm, have referred to this building as a "jewel of the Venetian Renaissance."

BIBLIOGRAPHY: *Semenzato 1964; McAndrew 1983, pp. 152 ff.*

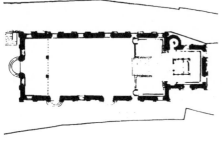

56

Corner Chapel
in the Church of the Santi Apostoli
1483-1499
Mauro Codussi
Cannaregio, Campo dei Santi Apostoli
Actv: Ca' d'Oro vaporetto stop

Sole and significant survivor of the general 15th-century renovation is the chapel built for the family of the Queen of Cyprus, Caterina Cornaro. The interior appears as a dome set on four corner columns, while from outside it seems like a cube joined to a hemisphere.

BIBLIOGRAPHY: *Puppi-Olivato 1977, pp. 230 ff.*

57

Scuola of San Giovanni Evangelista
1454-1512
Pietro Lombardo and Mauro Codussi
San Polo 2454, Campiello della Scuola
Actv: San Tomà vaporetto stop

At the beginning of the 14th century, the Confraternity of the Battuti moved to this area, perhaps to a hospice of the Badoer. Not until the middle of the 15th century was the confraternity able to build its own building, adjacent to the church of San Giovanni Evangelista. After 1454, the side façade with ogee windows took shape; then, from 1475 to 1481, Pietro Lombardo oversaw the construction of the distinctive marble frame which joins the opposed fronts, so as to describe a homogeneous space. The work done by Codussi (after 1498) probably included the portal and the interior stairway, which leads to the grand hall, definitively completed in its current state in the 18th century.

BIBLIOGRAPHY: *Pignatti 1981, pp. 41 ff.; McAndrew 1983, pp. 146 ff.*

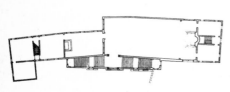

58

Palazzo Dario
1487-1492
Dorsoduro 352, Campiello Barbaro
Actv: Salute vaporetto stop

Described by McAndrew as a "a typical palazzo," this building as a whole seems to be linked to the traditional local style, while the details seem to be products of the Renaissance. This can probably be attributed to the circle of the Lombardos (a dynasty of craftsmen/architects), evidently quite skilled in assembling polychrome marble. The front overlooking the garden has a number of late-Gothic features.

BIBLIOGRAPHY: *Lieberman 1982, plate 16; McAndrew 1983, p. 213*

59

Scuola Grande of San Marco
1485-1495
Pietro Lombardo and Mauro Codussi
Castello 6778, Campo SS. Giovanni e Paolo
Actv: Fondamente Nuove or Ospedale vaporetto stop

Building began under the direction of Pietro Lombardo, but in 1490 Mauro Codussi replaced him. Codussi was responsible for designing, in the main façade, the curvilinear crown, perhaps inspired by the large arches of Saint Mark's. The lower part of the elevation was by the Lombardos,

on the other hand, and their imaginative approach and decorative skill can be clearly recognized. In its asymmetrical structure, the façade reflects the structure of the interior: to the right is the *albergo* (small meeting room) on the upper floor, and on the left is the *salone* (chapel). Through the entry portal (attributed to Giovanni Buora) one can now reach the wards of the City Hospital, which occupy the cloisters of the former Dominican convent.

BIBLIOGRAPHY: *Puppi-Olivato 1977, pp. 196 ff.; Pignatti 1981, pp. 129 ff.*

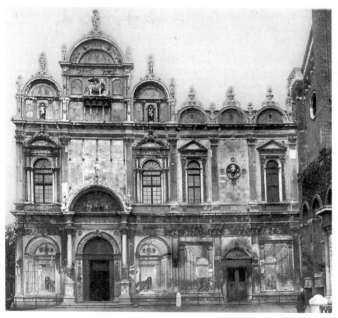

60

Palazzo Contarini dal Zaffo near San Vio
circa 1490
Dorsoduro 875, Calle Rota
Actv: Accademia vaporetto stop

This building has been attributed to a number of different architects (Codussi, Pietro Lombardo, Buora); in the front that overlooks the Grand Canal, the two pentaforate windows with semi-circular arches stand out. Praised by Ruskin, polychrome decorations and linings appear here in far more measured forms than in other Lombardesque structures from the late 15th century.

BIBLIOGRAPHY: *Bassi 1976, pp. 94 ff.; Puppi-Olivato 1977, pp. 236 ff.*

61

Church of Santa Maria Formosa
1492, 1604
Mauro Codussi
Castello, Campo Santa Maria Formosa
Actv: Rialto or San Zaccaria vaporetto stop

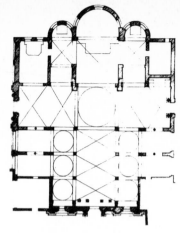

In terms of purity of conception and line, this may be – of all of Codussi's churches – the one that most closely approaches the architectural models of central Italy. This is particularly notable on the interior, where the timber ribbing emphasizes the structure. The Latin-cross plan may reflect a medieval structure (this church was founded in the 7th century). The exterior fronts seem to be far less unified in style and compo-

sition; they are isolated on all four sides, and can therefore be seen practically in their entirety. The elevation overlooking the Rio is from the 16th-century, and may have been designed by Codussi; the parts that overlook the Campo date from 1604. The bell tower is also from the 17th century.

BIBLIOGRAPHY: Puppi-Olivato 1977, p. 206; McAndrew 1983

62

Church of San Giovanni Crisostomo
1497-1504
Mauro Codussi
Cannaregio, Salizzada San Giovanni Crisostomo
Actv: Rialto vaporetto stop

Codussi here designed his usual tripartite façade, with curvilinear crown, in plaster, and not in stone. The interior, on a Greek-cross plan and with a dome in the center, was to become a model, based on those qualities of sober construction found in Santa Maria Formosa. The precious decorative elements of the chapels stand out on the bare surfaces.

BIBLIOGRAPHY: Puppi-Olivato 1977; McAndrew 1983

63

Palazzo Corner Spinelli

circa 1490
Mauro Codussi
San Marco 3877, Campiello del Teatro
Actv: Sant'Angelo vaporetto stop

On the façade overlooking the Grand Canal, Codussi developed an architectural scheme based on repetition, in a double order, of a special type of biforate window. It had a blind oculus and a semicircular ribbing enclosed it, in line with an overall design that seems to harmonize late-Gothic and Renaissance features.

BIBLIOGRAPHY: *Puppi-Olivato 1977, pp. 203 ff.; Gemin-Pedrocco 1990*

64

Palazzo Vendramin Calergi

between 1481 and 1509
Mauro Codussi
Cannaregio 2040, Campiello Vendramin
Actv: San Marcuola vaporetto stop

In this building overlooking the Grand Canal, Codussi refined and applied on a grand scale the architectural scheme previously developed for Palazzo Corner Spinelli: arranged in a double order, the sequence of biforate windows is punctuated by both single and paired semico-lumns; the windows appear to be set between solid cornices. In this late work, Codussi shows a remarkable mastery of the classical language; unlike with other architects of the early Venetian Renaissance, this sets Codussi apart from his origins as a builder. Completed after 1504 by the Lombardos, and in the early 17th century by Vincenzo Scamozzi, the palazzo, with its spectacular interiors, is the winter location of the city Casino.

BIBLIOGRAPHY: *Mariacher 1965; Puppi-Olivato 1977, pp. 221 ff.*

65

Clock Tower

1496-1506
Mauro Codussi and Pietro Lombardo
Saint Mark's Square
Actv: San Marco or San Zaccaria vaporetto stop

Above the large archway that leads to the Mercerie, Codussi built a tower in which there appear, in balanced succession, a number of evocative features: the mechanical clock, a niche with a statue of the Virgin, the lion of Saint Mark, the bell of the Moors. The two side wings were erected subsequently, under the direction of Pietro Lombardo.

BIBLIOGRAPHY: *Puppi-Olivato 1977, pp. 208 ff.; McAndrew 1983, pp. 355 ff.*

66

Procuratie Vecchie

1500-1532
Saint Mark's Square, north side
Actv: San Marco or San Zaccaria vaporetto stop

Hearkening back to Veneto-Byzantine tradition, the architect established a prototype with a double order of semicircular openings, set above a portico of fifty arches, intended for use as *botteghe* (shops). With its length of nearly five hundred feet, the building encloses the north side of the square. Traditionally, the building was attributed to Codussi; today critical opinion tends to veer toward Scarpagnino.

BIBLIOGRAPHY: *Puppi-Olivato 1977, pp. 211 ff.*

67

Dormitory of the Benedictine Convent of San Giorgio Maggiore

1496-1507
Guglielmo Buora
Island of San Giorgio
Actv: San Giorgio vaporetto stop

This corresponds to the oldest, eastern part of the convent complex (see entries nos. 113, 114), and it encloses the courtyard of the Allori (laurels). It is also called the *manica lunga* (long sleeve); it stretches behind the church for a good four hundred feet. The long rectangle is concluded to the north, toward the Riva degli Schiavoni, by a small façade with three semicircular frontons.

BIBLIOGRAPHY: *Lieberman 1982; McAndrew 1983, p. 459*

68
East Wing of the Doge's Palace
1483-1498
Antonio Rizzo
Piazza San Marco
Actv: San Marco or San Zaccaria vaporetto stop

After the fire of 1483, the Veronese sculptor and "protomagistro," Antonio Rizzo, was entrusted with the reconstruction of the part of the palazzo, between the Rio and the courtyard, which contained the offices of the magistrates and the living quarters of the Doge. On the interior, he set a façade above the basement, with two orders of centered windows of varying height (the multicolored marble decoration was added by the Lombardos after 1498). Rizzo was also responsible for the severe elevation overlooking the Rio. To provide access to the loggia on the first floor, the Scala dei Giganti was built; aligned with the lavishly decorated Arco of the Foscari (1471), this constitutes a sort of *via triumphalis* for the Doge's court. Beyond the stairway is the small courtyard of the Senators, the back façades to which were later built to designs by Spavento and Scarpagnino.

BIBLIOGRAPHY: *McAndrew 1983, p. 91; Franzoi 1990*

69
Marciana Sacristy and San Teodoro Chapel
1486-1491
Giorgio Spavento
Saint Mark's Square
Actv: San Marco or San Zaccaria vaporetto stop

This sacristy was conceived as a terminal element to the apse, located midway between the Doge's Palace, and the Palazzo Patriarcale (Patriarch's Palace). Spavento planned it as an independent structure with a vaulted ceiling set on tall abutments. Alongside it is the chapel, a simple hall ending in an apse.

BIBLIOGRAPHY: *Franzoi-Di Stefano 1976, p. 311; McAndrew 1983, pp. 400 ff.*

70

Palazzo Grimani near San Polo
circa 1500
San Polo 2033, Ramo Grimani
Actv: San Tomà vaporetto stop

The elevation overlooking the Grand Canal offers a significant example of late-Lombardesque architecture. On a monochrome background, the windows with pediment stand out; above them are pairs of triforate windows flanked by rounded-arch openings.

BIBLIOGRAPHY: Bassi 1976, pp. 418 ff.

71

Palazzo Zorzi near San Severo
circa 1500
Mauro Codussi
Castello 4930, Salizzada Zorzi
Actv: San Zaccaria vaporetto stop

This is one of Codussi's last works, and it is quite original. In particular, the long façade overlooking Rio di San Severo is marked horizontally by strips of Istrian stone, which are in turn separated at intervals by balaustrades and tondi. Of note are also the entry portal and in the spacious courtyard the portal which contains the well.

BIBLIOGRAPHY: Bassi 1976, pp. 558 ff.; McAndrew 1983, pp. 303 ff.

72

Palazzo Trevisan Cappello
circa 1500
Castello 4330, Ponte della Canonica
Actv: San Zaccaria vaporetto stop

Attributed by some to the Lombardos and by others to Bartolomeo Bon, this building offers, in its elevation, the usual repertory of proto-Renaissance features, including polyforate windows, with semicircular arches and marble decorations. In the plan, there are two independent residences, unified only by the façade.

BIBLIOGRAPHY: Angelini 1961, pp. 37 ff.; Bassi 1976, pp. 242 ff.

73

Palazzo Malipiero Trevisan

circa 1510

Castello 5250, Campo Santa Maria Formosa

Actv: Rialto or San Zaccaria vaporetto stop

An example of late Lombardesque architecture, this building has been attributed to the circle of the Lombardos (and by some to Sante Lombardo). The façade overlooking the Campo is laid out according to a symmetrical structure around the two central quadriforate windows. Here, as in other similar cases, the centered windows, set on slender pillars, predominate.

BIBLIOGRAPHY: *Bassi 1976*, pp. 493 ff.; *Puppi-Olivato 1977*, pp. 240 ff.

74

Palazzo Contarini dalle Figure

after 1504

San Marco 3327, Calle Mocenigo

Actv: San Samuele vaporetto stop

Traditionally attributed to Scarpagnino, this palazzo overlooks the Grand Canal with a stone façade, only partly in conformity with the models of the Lombardos. Above the polyforate window of the first floor, there is an elongated tympanum and, on either side, reliefs of weapons and coats-of-arms. The owner, Jacopo Contarini, allowed Andrea Palladio to live there for many years.

BIBLIOGRAPHY: *Bassi 1976*, pp. 382 ff.

75

Palazzo Michiel
near the Madonna dell'Orto

after 1503

Giovanni Buora

Cannaregio 3218, Fondamenta della Sensa

Actv: Madonna dell'Orto vaporetto stop

In this building, and in particular, on the façade overlooking the Rio, we can see clear signs of 16th-century architecture. See the *piano nobile* emphasized by special architraves and the corner pilasters of the superimposed type. The rustication is found only at the basement level, while the upper framed surfaces are in plaster.

BIBLIOGRAPHY: *Bassi 1976*, pp. 444 ff.

76

Church and Scuoletta of San Rocco
1489-1508
Bartolomeo Bon
San Polo, Campo San Rocco

Actv: San Tomà vaporetto stop

The 18th-century renovation, by Scalfarotto, modified the interior only in part, affecting one aisle; otherwise, the apsidal chapels and other areas offer a significant array of 15th- and 16th-century decorative features. The monumental façade (1765-1771) contrasts with the unassuming simplicity of the Scuoletta (on the left).

BIBLIOGRAPHY: *Angelini 1961, pp. 37 ff.; McAndrew 1983, pp. 468 ff.*

77

Scuola of San Giorgio degli Schiavoni
after 1500
Castello 3253, Calle dei Furlani

Actv: Arsenale vaporetto stop

This building of the Dalmatian community is known particular for the series of *teleri* (hanging paintings) executed by Carpaccio. The interior still has the personality of a small late-14th-century Scuola, split up between *sala* and *albergo*. The handsome tripartite façade (by G. De Zan, circa 1550) recalls Sansovino's elevation of the church of San Geminiano, since destroyed.

BIBLIOGRAPHY: *Pignatti 1981, pp. 99 ff.*

78

Church of Santa Maria Mater Domini
1502-1540
Santa Croce, Campo Santa Maria Mater Domini

Actv: San Stae vaporetto stop

The names of Buora and Sansovino (the latter for the façade) have been mentioned in connection with this small and elegant building. In the layout used, a Greek-cross plan with a dome at the intersection of the naves, there are features of the 15th and 16th century, linked both to local models (Byzantine cube) and to Renaissance examples, brought in from elsewhere.

BIBLIOGRAPHY: *Tramontin 1962; Franzoi-Di Stefano 1976, pp. 60 ff.*

79

Church of San Salvador

1507-1534

Giorgio Spavento and Tullio Lombardo

San Marco, Merceria and Campo San Salvador

Actv: Rialto vaporetto stop

According to tradition, this is one of the three oldest churches in the city (7th century). Spavento rebuilt it on the outline of a 12th-century structure, and in so doing he chose to hearken back to tradition and adopted a Byzantine model in which domes and arches succeed one another, as in Saint Mark's. After 1520, Tullio Lombardo completed the aisles; last of all came Sansovino, working on a building that had by this point taken on the characteristics of the full Renaissance. This church is located in the very heart of Venice, and is hemmed in by the surrounding buildings. The sole exception to this is the façade, which overlooks the Campo, rebuilt in Baroque forms by Giuseppe Sardi in 1663. Between the church and the Rio are the two large courtyards of the adjacent convent.

BIBLIOGRAPHY: McAndrew 1983, pp. 419 ff.; Tafuri 1985, pp. 24 ff.; Concina 1988

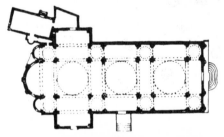

80

Church of Santa Maria della Visitazione

1494-1524

Dorsoduro, Zattere ai Gesuati

Actv: Zattere vaporetto stop

Reconstruction of an early 15th-century oratory, this building appears with Lombardesque shapes that can be traced to the circle of Codussi (in this connection, one should note the portal). On the interior, which can be reached from the professional school to which the church now belongs, a triumphal arch gives access to the presbytery, covered by a blind dome.

BIBLIOGRAPHY: Lorenzetti 1963, pp. 527 ff.; Franzoi-Di Stefano 1976, p. 207

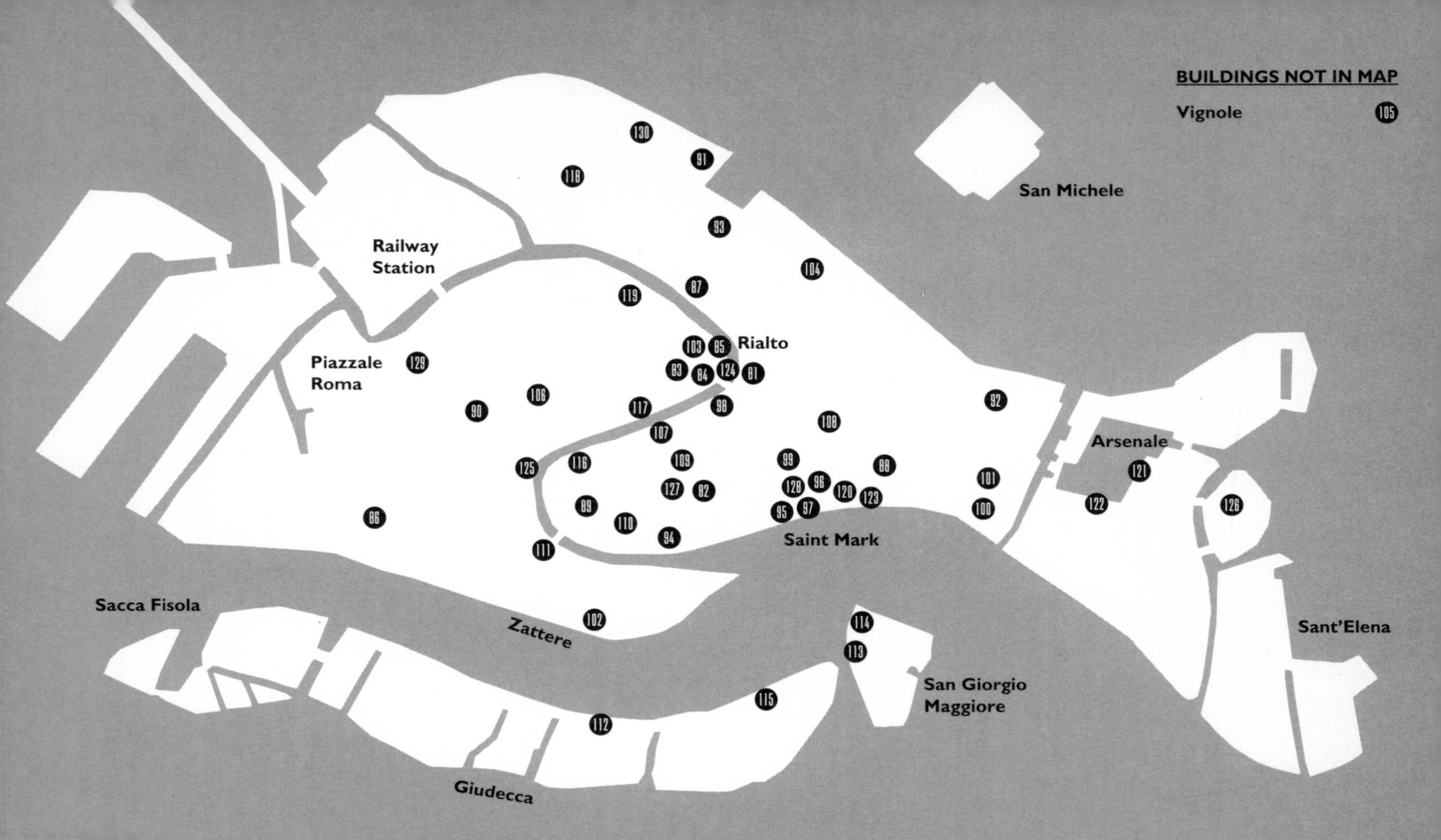

BUILDINGS NOT IN MAP
Vignole 105

San Michele

Vignole

San Giorgio Maggiore

Sant'Elena

Arsenale

Saint Mark

Rialto

Railway Station

Piazzale Roma

Zattere

Giudecca

Sacca Fisola

Sixteenth-Century Venice

In this phase, a great many of the most significant events took place, revolving around a few crucial areas, their architectural transformation, and their functional modification: the zone around the market of Rialto, rebuilt by the supervisor of works (proto) Scarpagnino. The manufacturing district: l'Arsenale. And the most important area for the display of prestige: Saint Mark's Square. Jacopo Sansovino was one of the chief architects of this transformation. He arrived from Rome in 1527, and immediately became a major figure in Venice as the first truly modern architect: not an expert who learned everything from the construction yards, but an intellectual who had developed through his studies of the modern classics. The Mint, the Loggetta, the Marciana National Library (and later the Procuratie Nuove) constitute the first examples of the full Renaissance which began to develop, late and despite many hindrances, on the lagoon. The delay was a result not only of competition with Florence and Rome, but also with Milan and Padua; the hindrances can be sensed in the interruptions in projects by Sansovino and Palladio, including the plan for the bridge of Rialto. Last in chronological sequence, among the various important episodes of the Venetian Renaissance, was the renovation of the Benedictine complex that stands on the Island of San Giorgio, and which serves as a visual counterweight to the buildings of Saint Mark's Square; Andrea Palladio was to work here, another architect in the fullest sense of the word.

81

Fondaco dei Tedeschi
1505-1508
Giorgio Spavento and Scarpagnino
San Marco 5342, Salizzada del Fontego
Actv: Rialto vaporetto stop

This massive, square building, once a warehouse used by German merchants to store their goods, was rebuilt after burning down. In 1939, it became Venice's main post office; even in its modern function it kept its original structure, facing inward, with four porticoed façades overlooking the central courtyard. The façade on the Grand Canal was originally frescoed by Giorgione.
BIBLIOGRAPHY: *Brunetti-Dazzi 1941; McAndrew 1983, pp. 405 ff.*

82

Church of San Fantin
1507-1564
Sebastiano da Lugano and Scarpagnino
San Marco, Campo San Fantin
Actv: Santa Maria del Giglio or San Marco vaporetto stop

In this church, built with the bequest of Cardinal Zen, the architectural structure of the Church of San Salvador reappears; here, however, the structure has been simplified, with three cross vaults instead of three domes; only the presbytery, added later and attributed by some to Sansovino, is covered by a dome.
BIBLIOGRAPHY: *Franzoi-Di Stefano 1976, pp. 322 ff.; Vio 1977*

83

Church of San Giovanni Elemosinario
1527-1539
Scarpagnino
San Polo, Ruga Rialto
Actv: San Silvestro or Rialto vaporetto stop

The church, hidden in the building fabric, was part of the reconstruction of Rialto. Scarpagnino designed it in the form of a square, within which is inscribed a central dome set on a fan vault, and four arms of the plan, covered by barrel vaults. Here, too, as in the Church of San Salvador, we find a structure borrowed from Byzantine models, and in particular from Saint Mark's.
BIBLIOGRAPHY: *Calabi-Morachiello 1985; Calabi 1987, pp. 100 ff.*

84

Fabbriche Vecchie of Rialto
1520-1522
Scarpagnino
San Polo, marketplace of Rialto

Actv: San Silvestro or Rialto vaporetto stop

With the exception of the church of San Gia-cometto, all of the buildings on the marketplace of Rialto burned in the fire of January 1514. A few months later, the plan by the Proto Scarpagnino was chosen from the seven competing designs. Scarpagnino's plan adhered to the existing floor plan.

Employing a simplified classical idiom, the design comprises a homogeneous structure governed by a uniform height, linked by the continuity of porticoes and cornices. At street level, the disposition of the architectural volumes establishes spaces linked to specific activities (Erbaria, greengrocery; Pescaria, fishmongery; Portico del Bancogiro, banking; Drapperia, upholstery); on the upper floors are administrative offices, and in particular the offices of the magistracy.

BIBLIOGRAPHY: *Calabi-Morachiello 1984; Calabi 1987,* pp. 61 ff.

85

Palazzo dei Camerlenghi
1525-1528
Scarpagnino
San Polo, at the foot of the bridge of Rialto

Actv: San Silvestro or Rialto vaporetto stop

As if to set a seal of completion upon the rebuilding of Rialto, this white building made of Istrian stone unified three existing functions (prison, loggia of the merchants, and head-quarters of the Camerlenghi in a single structure. The palazzo, now the Administrative Courts building, was to serve as the central meeting point of the marketplace and its administrative jurisdiction.

BIBLIOGRAPHY: *Calabi-Morachiello 1984,* pp. 306 ff.

86

Church of San Sebastiano
1505-1548
Scarpagnino
Dorsoduro, Campo San Sebastiano
Actv: San Basilio vaporetto stop

The floor plan and the volumetric conception of this church is crystalline. Of particular renown are the frescoes by Paolo Veronese (1555-1565). Both the ceiling and the walls are divided up into squares and compartments in the overall shape of a Latin cross, with a single aisle and a domed presbytery. The hanging choir set above the atrium is particularly noteworthy.
BIBLIOGRAPHY: *Franzoi-Di Stefano 1976, pp. 182 ff.*

87

Church of San Felice
after 1530
Cannaregio, Strada Nuova
Actv: San Marcuola or Ca' d'Oro vaporetto stops

The building is attributed to one of the Proti in the circle of Codussi or the Lombardos (Sante has been mentioned); the plan reproduces the "cube" of Saint Mark's, which had already been used in other 15th- and 16th-century buildings. The form, in fact, is that of a square in which a Greek cross and a hemispheric dome are inscribed.
BIBLIOGRAPHY: *Franzoi-Di Stefano 1976, pp. 144 ff.*

88

Church of San Giorgio dei Greci
1539-1561
Sante Lombardo and others
Castello, Rio dei Greci
Actv: San Zaccaria vaporetto stop

This Orthodox church is part of series of landholdings that the Republic of Venice recognized as belonging to the Greek community. Of particular note are the three-part façade and the floor plan, with a single aisle and a dome in the center. At one extremity is a pensile choir, at the other is the presbytery, set off by an iconostasis (see entry no. 152).
BIBLIOGRAPHY: *Franzoi-Di Stefano 1976, pp. 479 ff.*

89
Palazzo Loredan at Santo Stefano
after 1536
Scarpagnino
San Marco 2945, Campo Santo Stefano
Actv: San Samuele or Accademia vaporetto stop
The well calibrated architecture of the elevation overlooking the Campo gives no hint of the spectacular atrium, which extends the full height and depth of the building. It features a stairway with a number of flights. This palazzo, today the seat of the Venetian Institute of Science, Literature, and Arts, was completed in 1618 by Giovanni Grapiglia, also responsible for the façade shaped in the Scamozzi's fashion on the shorter wall.
BIBLIOGRAPHY: Bassi 1976, pp. 255 ff.; Albertini 1985

90
Scuola Grande of San Rocco
1515-1560
Bartolomeo Bon, Scarpagnino, and Sante Lombardo
San Polo 3054, Campo San Rocco
Actv: San Tomà vaporetto stop
A succession of different Proti oversaw the construction of this building, owned by the confraternity of San Rocco. The Maestro Bon (1515-1524) was responsible for the overall plan of a rectangular hall surrounded by the stairwell.

He was also the designer of the lower floor with the Codussian biforate windows. Lombardo (1524-1527) was the designer of the façade overlooking the Rio, while Scarpagnino (1527-1549) completed the elevation overlooking the Campo. He is also considered to be the architect of the large staircase that leads to the two halls containing the immense series of paintings by Jacopo Tintoretto between 1564 and 1588.
BIBLIOGRAPHY: Pignatti 1981, pp. 151; Tafuri 1985, p. 125

91

Palazzo Contarini dal Zaffo
near the Misericordia
1530-1540
Cannaregio 3539, Fondamenta Contarini
Actv: Madonna dell'Orto vaporetto stop

This building was constructed at the order of Ga-
spare Contarini. Just beyond the building stand the
gardens, restored by the Johnston family at the
turn of the century. In part they still conserve the
appearance of a Venetian garden of the 16th
century. At the far end of the gardens, toward the
lagoon, stands the Casino degli Spiriti, which was
the setting for artistic and literary meetings.
BIBLIOGRAPHY: Brusatin 1988, pp. 211 ff.; Cunico
1989, pp. 130 ff.

92

Church of San Francesco della Vigna
1530-1572
Sansovino and Andrea Palladio
Castello, Campo San Francesco della Vigna
Actv: Celestia vaporetto stop

This was the first building designed and built by
Sansovino in Venice, the first example of a
piece of architecture that conforms to the standards of the mature Renaissance. The floor plan
reflects both the architectural principles of
ancient times and the Neo-Platonic ideals of
the Priore Francesco Zorzi, the author of a treatise on harmonious proportions. The central
dome has been eliminated, the side aisles have
been transformed into chapels, the presbytery has
been extended, and the various parts of the
church – in their starkly essential qualities – are
linked by proportional relationships based on the
number three (the width of the aisles, for example, corresponds to a third of their length). The
façade, on the other hand, was built after
1568, to a design by Palladio.
BIBLIOGRAPHY: *Wittkower 1964; Foscari-Tafuri 1983*

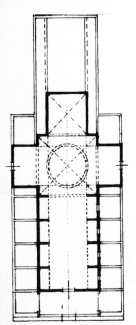

93

Scuola Grande of the Misericordia
1535-1583
Sansovino
Cannaregio 3555, Fondamenta dell'Abbazia
Actv: San Marcuola vaporetto stop

With its unfinished nature, the great building by Sansovino offers mute testimony to the great difficulties created, in 16th-century Venice, to a complete manifestation of the new architecture; neither the elevations nor the vaulted ceiling proposed by Sansovino were accepted, and in 1544 he abandoned the job.

BIBLIOGRAPHY: *Tafuri* 1985, pp. 143 ff.

94

Palazzo Corner near San Maurizio
1532-1561
Sansovino
San Marco 2661, Fondamenta Corner
Actv: Santa Maria del Giglio vaporetto stop

The impressive elevation overlooking the Grand Canal constitutes the first, spectacular expression of the new style in its most refined version. Just a few years previous, a similar design by Sansovino – done for another family with links of allegiance to the pope, the Grimani – had been turned down. Nonetheless, in this instance as well the building that Sansovino designed for the Corner family is meant to be an authentic "Roman-style" palazzo. This intention can be seen in the elevations (with rustication and with Ionic and Corinthian orders in sequences of paired columns), and it can also be seen in the floor plan, organized around a square courtyard. The building was later purchased by the city government, and since 1866 it has been used as the prefecture, or police courts.

BIBLIOGRAPHY: *Bassi* 1976, p. 88; *Tafuri* 1992, p. 328

95
Mint
1536-1545
Sansovino
Saint Mark's Wharf

Actv: San Marco or San Zaccaria vaporetto stop

When the plan for the new Mint was approved, it marked the beginning of a program for the renovation of Saint Mark's Square ordered by the Doge Andrea Gritti and conducted by Sansovino, in the official role of "proto supra le fab-

briche di San Marco." The façade overlooking the wharf originally stood two stories tall, and featured distinctive rustication, in conformity with the indications given by Sebastiano Serlio for utilitarian buildings in his treatise. The third story, where the motif of the rusticated half-columns is repeated, was added later by Sansovino himself. After the fall of the Republic of Venice, the Mint no longer served its original purpose, and it is now part of the Marciana National Library. BIBLIOGRAPHY: *Tafuri 1969, p. 72; Howard 1975, p. 38*

96
Loggetta of the Bell Tower
1537-1549
Sansovino
Saint Mark's Square

Actv: San Marco or San Zaccaria vaporetto stop

Originally intended as a guardhouse, this small building is aligned with the *via triumphalis* that leads through the Porta della Carta and terminates within the Doge's Palace. This is more a work of sculpture than it is a piece of architecture; it comprises three arcades of compound orders, adorned with a lavish set of decorative elements.
BIBLIOGRAPHY: *Howard 1975, pp. 28 ff.*

97
Marciana National Library
1537-1554
Sansovino
Piazzetta San Marco

Actv: San Marco or San Zaccaria vaporetto stop

This library was built to house a wealth of collections of volumes, including the library of Cardinal Bessarione, who fled Constantinople after it fell to the Turks. Sansovino designed it as an extended loggia, with a distinctive double order of half-columns. Atop an elaborate frieze with festoons he set an attic, of evident classical derivation, with a baluster and acroteria. This composition was later taken as a model for the south wing of Saint Mark's Square, known as the Procuratie Nuove. Inside, where the Marciana National Library is now housed, a monumental staircase leads to the Great Hall (26 × 10.5 meters), featuring a lavish array of gilded decorations, and a series of *tondi* by Paolo Veronese.

BIBLIOGRAPHY: Murray 1969, pp. 262 ff.; Howard 1975, pp. 8 ff.

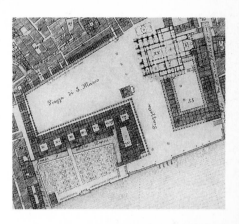

98
Palazzo Dolfin near San Salvador
1536-1545
Sansovino
San Marco 4799, Calle Larga Mazzini

Actv: Rialto vaporetto stop

During the same period in which he was redesigning Saint Mark's Square, Sansovino was remodelling the floor plan and the façades of this building, creating a hybrid version that mingled the existing with the new. The façade, in carved stone on the Grand Canal, is all that survives of Sansovino's original design; the building now houses the offices of the Bank of Italy.

BIBLIOGRAPHY: Bassi 1976, pp. 154 ff.; Tafuri 1992, pp. 316 ff.

99
Church of San Zulian
after 1553
Sansovino
San Marco, Campo San Zulian
Actv: San Zaccaria or Rialto vaporetto stop

This 9th-century building was rebuilt with funds provided by the physician and philosopher Tommaso Rangone, whose likeness can be seen in the lunette above the front door. Sansovino overlaid two distinct architectural frameworks here, creating a façade that borrowed much from commemorative architecture, with a double order of half-columns.

BIBLIOGRAPHY: *Tafuri 1969, pp. 141 ff.; Franzoi-Di Stefano 1976, pp. 363 ff.*

100
Ca' di Dio
1545-1570
Sansovino
Castello 2182, Riva di Ca' di Dio
Actv: Arsenale vaporetto stop

Originally designed to house pilgrims on their way to the Holy Land, this complex was used from the 14th century on as an oratory and hospice for poor and unwed women. When Sansovino set about renovating these structures, he designed façades so sober and austere as to prompt the author Manfredo Tafuri to speak of "architectural asceticism."

BIBLIOGRAPHY: *Franzoi-Di Stefano 1976, p. 498; Tafuri 1985, pp. 81 ff.*

101
Church of San Martino
near the Arsenale
1553-1633
Sansovino
Castello, Fondamenta del Piovan
Actv: Arsenale or Tana vaporetto stop

This building is traditionally linked to Ca' di Dio — Sansovino worked on it with similar intentions and with an equally austere architectural language. Here he transformed a medieval church built on a Latin-cross plan into a structure with a central plan, organized around a square, with two chapels on each side.

BIBLIOGRAPHY: *Howard 1975, pp. 77 ff.; Tafuri 1985, pp. 81 ff.*

102

Ospedale degli Incurabili

after 1565

Sansovino

Dorsoduro, Zattere agli Incurabili

Actv: Zattere or Salute vaporetto stop

The oratory and the hospice for the syphlitics had been arranged, ever since the Middle Ages, around a square courtyard. In redesigning them, Sansovino devoted special attention to the oratory, which he saw more as an auditorium where polyphonic concerts would be held, than as a place of worship. The church was demolished in 1831, and today all that survives is the hospice, with its distinctive array of decorations.

BIBLIOGRAPHY: *Howard 1975; Aikema-Meijers 1989*

103

Fabbriche Nuove of Rialto

1555-1556

Sansovino

San Polo 119, Erbaria

Actv: Rialto or San Silvestro vaporetto stop

Between the Erbaria and the Pescaria stands this building which reproduces the vertical design of the Fabbriche Vecchie, completing the reconstruction of Rialto along the Grand Canal. So different is this building in terms of style from Sansovino's other, better known works that – despite the reliable documentation showing him to be the architect – for many years it was considered to be by some other architect.

BIBLIOGRAPHY: *Tafuri 1969, p. 156; Calabi 1987, p. 142*

104

Palazzo Zen near the Crosecheri

1537-1553

Cannaregio 4922, Campo dei Gesuiti

Actv: Fondamente Nuove vaporetto stop

This singular building features a melange of Renaissance motifs and ogee arches of Eastern derivation; this is particularly evident in the elevation that faces Rio di Santa Caterina, in the alternating sequence of different styles. The building was designed by the owners, Venetian patricians in regular contact with Eastern art and culture.

BIBLIOGRAPHY: *Concina 1984/b*

105

Fortress of Sant'Andrea
1544-1571
Michele Sanmicheli
Island of the Vignole
Actv: Vígnole vaporetto stop

Originally known as Castelnuovo, this fort was the counterpart of the fortress of San Nicolò at Lido, in the system of defense guarding the mouths of the port of Venice. Sanmicheli did an extensive amount of work on military fortifications, as a consultant to the Republic of Venice; in that context, he designed this fort as a city gate, borrowing from the work done at Verona.
BIBLIOGRAPHY: Puppi 1971, pp. 87 ff.; Concina 1983, pp. 97 ff., 111 ff.

106

Palazzo Corner Mocenigo at San Polo
1559-1564
Michele Sanmicheli
San Polo 2128, Campo San Polo
Actv: San Tomà or San Silvestro vaporetto stop

Arranged in the shape of the letter "C," this palazzo turns its side toward the Campo and its front to the Rio di San Polo. Here, the impressive rustication of the basement, the two central large Serlian windows, and the tight rhythm in the placement of the pilaster strips give the composition an original flavor. This building is now the headquarters of the Financial Police.
BIBLIOGRAPHY: Puppi 1971, pp. 109 ff.; Bassi 1976, pp. 334 ff.

107

Palazzo Grimani near San Luca
1556-1575
Michele Sanmicheli
San Marco 4041, Calle Grimani
Actv: Rialto vaporetto stop

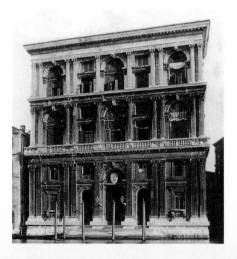

The façade, split into three great horizontal strips and divided by a continuous series of Serlian windows, is well known. Less familiar is the floor plan, by which the layout of Palazzo Corner (entry court; pòrtego, or elongated hall; and atrium, on the water) has been adapted to fit a trapezoidal area. The palazzo now houses the offices of the Venice Law Courts.
BIBLIOGRAPHY: Puppi 1971, pp. 136 ff.; Bassi 1976, pp. 146 ff.

108
Palazzo Grimani
near Santa Maria Formosa
1558-1569
Castello 4682, Ruga Giuffa
Actv: San Zaccaria or Rialto vaporetto stop

In the *ruga*, the only indication of this building's existence is the portal, which some scholars attribute to Sanmicheli; nor does the façade facing the Rio di San Severo give any hint of the lavish architecture and decorations to be found within. The interior was designed by the owner, the Patriarch of Aquileia, Giovanni Grimani, who housed his collections of ancient art here.
BIBLIOGRAPHY: Puppi 1971, p. 159; Bassi 1976, pp. 228 ff.

109
Palazzo Contarini near San Beneto
finished in 1560
San Marco 3980, Calle Contarini
Actv: Sant'Angelo vaporetto stop

Traditionally attributed to Sante Lombardo, this palazzo shows the earmarks of the period of transition, especially in the façade looking out over Rio di San Luca. The Serlian window of the *piano nobile* may smack of a more modern style, but a number of features are more typical of the early Renaissance, such as the use of polychrome marbles and the carved stone arches in the polyforate window on the top floor.
BIBLIOGRAPHY: Muraro 1970; Bassi 1976, pp. 258 ff.

110
Palazzo Bellavite at San Maurizio
completed in 1555
San Marco 2760, Campo San Maurizio
Actv: Santa Maria del Giglio vaporetto stop

In the façade looking out over the Campo, which once boasted frescoes by Paolo Veronese, one can see some of the features that later became a recurring model in aristocratic buildings in the late 16th century and the 17th century; this is particularly true of the two central Serlian windows, the elongated modillions, and the linking volutes.
BIBLIOGRAPHY: Bassi 1976, pp. 250 ff.

|||
Cloister of Santa Maria della Carità
1552
Andrea Palladio
Dorsoduro 1050, Campo della Carità
Actv: Accademia vaporetto stop

All that remains of Palladio's version is the wing between the courtyard and the Rio Terrà (the entire original plan is contained in the *Quattro Libri dell'Architettura*): in this part, now part of the Galleria dell'Accademia, we would point out in particular the interior elevation (with large arches set between half-columns), the corbelled oval staircase, and the complex hall of the Tablino.

BIBLIOGRAPHY: *Ackerman 1972, p. 74; Puppi 1973, p. 146*

|12
Church of the Redentore
1577-1592
Andrea Palladio
Giudecca, Fondamenta San Giacomo
Actv: Redentore vaporetto stop

This sanctuary, built after a tragic plague, towered over the surrounding buildings – one can see its bulk and the façade from afar, and Palladio meant it to appear as a sequence in perspective of different levels. The interior is split up into different sections, which correspond to different functions. The choir concerns the monastic function, the central body refers to the votive function, the nave and the chapels concern the parish function. This does nothing to prevent the creation of a single structure with a central arrangement, in which the longitudinal form with a single aisle is hemmed in by an arcade set on pillars. Light is provided through the central dome and the thermal windows that pierce the vaulted roof, along the nave and the presbytery.

BIBLIOGRAPHY: *Cevese 1973, pp. 89 ff.; Puppi 1973, pp. 210 ff., 419 ff.*

113

Refectory of San Giorgio Maggiore
1560-1563
Andrea Palladio
Island of San Giorgio
Actv: San Giorgio vaporetto stop

The reconstruction of the great Benedictine complex began toward 1540 with the renovation of the part that today corresponds to the refectory. Palladio completed it in 1563, and he conceived it as a sequence of three spaces leading the visitor from the vestibule to the great *salone* (called the Salone Palladiano), which is elongated, and covered by a cross-vault.

BIBLIOGRAPHY: *Cevese* 1973, p. 89; *Puppi* 1973, pp. 150 ff., 338 ff.

114

Church of San Giorgio Maggiore and Cloister of the Cipressi
from 1579 on
Andrea Palladio
Island of San Giorgio
Actv: San Giorgio vaporetto stop

This building was largely built after Palladio's death, and was completed in the 17th century. The plan called for a church that would be expanded and rebuilt according to a plan that swiveled 90° with respect to the previous plan.

In this case as well, the great extension lengthwise would do nothing to prevent the architectural structure from acquiring the status of a central-plan building, because of the importance of the dome in the overall composition. The façade, set on two separate orders, was built in 1610 by Simone Sorella. The large quadriporticus cloister, too, known as the Cloister of the Cypresses, was designed by Palladio but built after his death. The entire complex, since 1951, has been the headquarters of the Giorgio Cini Foundation.

BIBLIOGRAPHY: *Zorzi* 1966, p. 42; *Puppi* 1973, p. 158

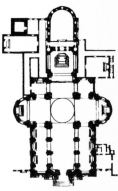

115

Church and Hospice of the Zitelle

1582-1586

Andrea Palladio and Jacopo Bozzetto

Giudecca, Fondamenta delle Zitelle

Actv: Zitelle vaporetto stop

According to tradition, this is the third church by Palladio in the Giudecca, and here too it was built after the architect's death. The square plan, with rounded corners, is almost entirely covered by the dome. With the hospice that surrounds it on three sides, the church constitutes a single architectural complex.

BIBLIOGRAPHY: Puppi 1973, pp. 431 ff.; Aikema-Meijers 1989, pp. 225 ff.

116

Palazzo Mocenigo near San Samuele

1570-1590

San Marco 3349, Calle Mocenigo

Actv: Sant'Angelo vaporetto stop

Part of a series of four palazzo overlooking the Grand Canal, this building was for many years, and mistakenly, attributed to Palladio. It is, instead, a clear expression of the manner that he so strongly influenced, particularly recognizable in several features, such as the curvilinear pediments above the side windows and the framed surfaces in stone in the lower part of the façade.

BIBLIOGRAPHY: Bassi 1976, pp. 134 ff.

117

Palazzo Tiepolo near Sant'Aponal

circa 1560

Guglielmo dei Grigi

San Polo 1364, Calle Papadopoli

Actv: San Silvestro vaporetto stop

The palazzo, which appears as a background in a painting by Paolo Veronese from 1571, seems to sum up a number of aspects of late 16th-century building, inspired by the work of Sanmicheli. Set between extremely pronounced cornices, the traditional three-part composition is here punctuated at the center by Serlian motif windows, set one atop another.

BIBLIOGRAPHY: Bassi 1976, pp. 140 ff.

118

Ghetto Nuovo
from 1516 on
Cannaregio, Campo del Ghetto Nuovo
Actv: San Marcuola vaporetto stop

A decree of 1516 forced the Jewish community to reside on the "island," which is to say, along the Rio di San Gerolamo, already the site of a foundry where the *geto* or *ghetto*, meaning "casting," or copper was done. The high concentration of inhabitants, along with the requirement of keeping a central space free, is the reason for the characteristic volumetric configuration whereby the buildings rose and crowded together only along the external perimeter. The synagogues (Scuole), too, community meeting places and places of worship, are set around the Campo, and fit right into the array of build-

ings; introspective architecture reveal surprising decorative richness. This is the case with the Scuola Grande Tedesca [1], the Scuola Canton [2] (both of them erected in 1528-1532), and lastly with the Scuola Italiana [3] (1581-1587).
BIBLIOGRAPHY: *Gianighian 1984, pp. 186 ff.; Concina 1991, pp. 11 ff., 93 ff.; Calabi 1991/a pp. 217 ff.*

119

Palazzo Tron near San Stae
1570-1580
Santa Croce, 1947, Corte Dandolo
Actv: San Stae vaporetto stop

The façade overlooking the Canal Grande in particular shows the influence of Sansovino: in the center are the balustered quadriforate windows, enriched by such details as elongated modillions and cornices in relief. Although it bears similar motifs, the front overlooking the garden is the product of 18th-century renovations. The building today houses the offices of the urban-planning department of the University Institute of Architecture.
BIBLIOGRAPHY: *Bassi 1976, pp. 190 ff.*

120

Prisons

1563-1614

Antonio Da Ponte and Antonio Contin

San Marco, Ponte della Paglia

Actv: San Zaccaria vaporetto stop

This building faces the Doge's Palace, directly across the Rio, at the mouth of the Riva degli Schiavoni. Construction was begun by Giovanni Antonio Rusconi, and was designed by Da Ponte in sober and classical forms that echo the proportions and rustication of its more aristocratic sisters in Saint Mark's Square. Contin completed the structure in the 17th century.

BIBLIOGRAPHY: *Bassi 1962, pp. 64 ff.; Franzoi 1990, pp. 111 ff.*

121

Shipyards known as "Cantieri delle Gagiandre"

1568-1585

Castello, Darsena dell'Arsenale Novissimo

Actv: Arsenale or Tana vaporetto stop

These *squeri all'acqua* were designed immediately following the Battle of Lepanto to house a fleet of galleys ready to start at a moment's notice, and they were part of a larger reorganization of the Arsenale. The building's dignified architecture, punctuated by large arches on Istrian stone columns, has suggested to many scholars that Sansovino may have designed it.

BIBLIOGRAPHY: *Concina 1984/b, pp. 154 ff.*

122

Rope Works of the Tana

1579-1591

Antonio Da Ponte

Castello, Campo della Tana

Actv: Tana vaporetto stop

This very long building, now used for temporary exhibitions, was built on the remains of an earlier building, designed for the manufacture of rope and cable. The new factory for processing hemp was built by the Proto Da Ponte designed with functional and manufacturing requirements in mind; at the center the structure is a single space from top to bottom, while along the sides it is split up into a first and second floor.

BIBLIOGRAPHY: *Concina 1984/b, pp. 158 ff.*

123
Bridge of Sighs
1595-1600
Scarpagnino
San Marco, Rio di Palazzo
Actv: San Zaccaria vaporetto stop

The need for direct communications between the prison and the Doge's Palace was the reason for the construction of this very well known bridge, made of Istrian stone and designed by the Proto of the Doge's Palace, with a great wealth of decorative sculpture. Several details link it to the bridge of the Guglie, built at the same time, and set at the mouth of the canal of Cannaregio.

BIBLIOGRAPHY: *Bassi 1962, p. 66; Franzoi 1990, p. 112*

124
Rialto Bridge
1588-1591
Antonio Da Ponte
* Rialto vaporetto stop

This bridge, in its current, unmistakable appearance, is the product of a long debate, which began in 1514 and went on for seventy years, following the collapse of the previous wooden bridge. Tradition has it that the greatest architects of the time contributed to the definition of the model used (Vasari even mentions Michelangelo in this connection). Palladio presented a series of designs for a bridge with several arches "in the manner of the ancients," but they were not accepted. One or three arches – in the end the debate turned on these alternatives, and the Venetian Senate chose the first solution, preferring the design by the Proto Antonio Da Ponte to the more authoritative model by Scamozzi.

BIBLIOGRAPHY: *Morachiello 1987*

125

Palazzo Balbi near San Tomà
1582-1590
Alessandro Vittoria
Dorsoduro 3901, Calle del Remer
Actv: San Tomà vaporetto stop

Indicated as a sign of the transition to Baroque, this palazzo offers, in the elevation overlooking the Grand Canal, a synthesis of the architectural features of the 16th century: the polyforate window with baluster, in the manner of Sansovino, the broken pediments in the style of Palladio, all of which are linked to a lavish decorative approach. The building is now the headquarters of the Government of the Region of Venetia.
BIBLIOGRAPHY: *Bassi 1976, pp. 124 ff.*

126

Church of San Pietro di Castello
1557-1596, 1619-1621
Francesco Smeraldi and Giovanni Girolamo Grapiglia
Castello, Campo San Pietro
Actv: Giardini or Arsenale vaporetto stop

This church stands on the remains of a church dating from the 17th century. Though it is set at the farthest reaches of Castello, it was the Cathedral of Venice from 1451 to 1807. It echoes certain Palladian features, both in the double framed façade and in the Latin-cross plan of the interior, with the central dome. The bell tower was built by Codussi in 1482-1488.
BIBLIOGRAPHY: *Puppi 1973, pp. 345 ff.*

127

Scuola of San Fantin
1592-1600
Antonio Contin
San Marco 1897, Campo San Fantin
Actv: Santa Maria del Giglio or San Marco vaporetto stop

With its white, somewhat chalky façade made of Istrian stone, the Scuola seems to be an early expression of Baroque art. The sculptural impulse that seems to inform it may perhaps be attributed to Alessandro Vittoria, who promoted the project. The two halls (on the ground floor and on the upper floor) are now at the disposal of the Ateneo Veneto, which has had its offices here since 1811.
BIBLIOGRAPHY: *Pignatti 1981, pp. 187 ff.*

128

Procuratie Nuove
1586-1616
Vincenzo Scamozzi
Saint Mark's Square
Actv: San Marco or San Zaccaria vaporetto stop
Along the southern side of the square, Scamozzi conceived the new wing as an extension

of the Marciana National Library, whose horizontal and vertical modules it copies. The third floor is slightly set back so as not to compromise the architectural unity and stylistic continuity of the elevations. Scamozzi built ten arches of this building, while the rest was the work of Longhena.
BIBLIOGRAPHY: *Bassi 1962, pp.* 109 ff.

129

Church and Convent of San Nicolò da Tolentino
1591-1602
Vincenzo Scamozzi
Santa Croce, Campo dei Tolentini
Actv: Piazzale Roma vaporetto stop

In its overall plan and structure, this church of the Teatini echoes the Palladian model of a Latin cross and central dome; set upon the bare façade is a large colonnaded pronaos, built by Andrea Tirali in 1706-1714 in the form of a Corinthian temple. Today the convent contains the University Institute of Architecture (see entry no. 245).
BIBLIOGRAPHY: *Bassi 1962, pp.* 269 ff.

130

Palazzo Benci near the Madonna dell'Orto
1580-1590
Cannaregio 3458, Fondamenta della Madonna dell'Orto
Actv: Madonna dell'Orto vaporetto stop

This huge complex, which now houses a convalescent home, was intended to incorporate two existing buildings, but was never completed (the Gothic façade still looks out over the Fondamenta). The front overlooking the courtyard gives an idea of the size of the project; in the garden, the two symmetrical blocks constituted a backdrop and served as the "Casino degli Spiriti."
BIBLIOGRAPHY: *Bassi 1976, pp.* 308 ff.

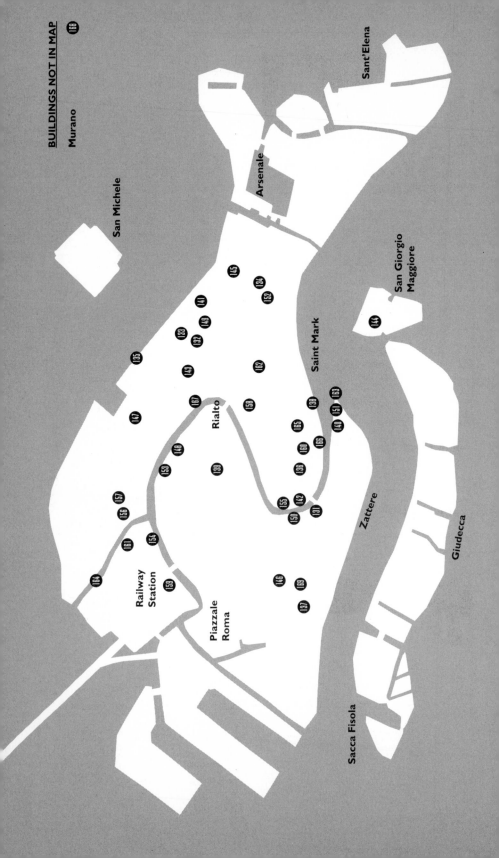

Baroque Venice

17th-century Venice was not blessed with personalities on a par with those of the previous, nor of the following, century. In part because of this paucity of talent, and in part because of the relative scarcity of new building in this period, the notion of Baroque does not really make a full-fledged appearance in the city's artistic history. Only a very few buildings, and those restricted to the work of Gaspari, reveal stylistic references to the Roman models by Bernini and Borromini, traditionally considered to be the heart of Baroque.

In a marked contrast with other eras, however, a single figure towers over the others – Baldassare Longhena, an architect who was born and raised in Venice. With its spectacular central plan, his Church of the Salute remains one of the greatest monuments of the 17th century (according to Deborah Howard, the greatest outside of Rome). Longhena left his mark especially in the civil architecture, establishing completely new features. He is responsible for the continuous sequence of windows that breaks the three-part rhythm of the Venetian palazzo. In Ca' Pesaro and in Ca' Rezzonico, he returned to the motif of the double order, invented by Sansovino and carried forward by his teacher Vincenzo Scamozzi, in the Procuratie Nuove.

If we can speak at all of the Baroque in Venice, we can only do so in terms of a continuity that links the architecture of the 16th century with that of Longhena.

131

Palazzo Contarini degli Scrigni
1609
Vincenzo Scamozzi
Dorsoduro 1057, Calle Contarini Corfù
Actv: Accademia vaporetto stop

This building was an expansion of the nearby Gothic palazzo; what stands out in the new elevation overlooking the Grand Canal is the regularity of the architectural motif in which the centered window is balanced against a set of paired columns. This is a clearly Baroque layout that makes brilliant use of the models of the 16th-century masters.

BIBLIOGRAPHY: *Bassi 1976, pp. 98 ff.*

132

Ospedale dei Mendicanti
1601-1631
Vincenzo Scamozzi
Castello, Fondamenta dei Mendicanti
Actv: Ospedale or Fondamente Nuove vaporetto stop

This complex is arrayed, in a perfectly symmetrical manner, around two square courtyards; the church (see entry no. 133), located in the center, acts as the axis of symmetry. The building, originally intended to house orphans and vagabonds, is now part of the city hospital, of which it constitutes the third and fourth courtyard, from the main entry.

BIBLIOGRAPHY: *Aikema-Mejers 1989, pp. 249 ff.; Concina 1989, pp. 123 ff.*

133

Church of San Lazzaro dei Mendicanti
1601-1649
Vincenzo Scamozzi and Giuseppe Sardi
Castello, Fondamenta dei Mendicanti
Actv: Ospedale or Fondamente Nuove vaporetto stop

The layout is in part borrowed from Sansovino's model for the Incurabili, but is modified with a view to a number of Palladian examples. Flanked by four lateral altars, the single aisle is preceded by a vestibule which, in turn, serves as funerary chapel. The vaulted ceiling has large thermal windows.

BIBLIOGRAPHY: *Franzoi-Di Stefano 1976, pp. 442 ff.; Pellegriti 1989*

134

Church of San Lorenzo

1592-1617
Simone Sorella
Castello, Campo San Lorenzo

Actv: San Zaccaria or Arsenale vaporetto stop

Extremely ancient in origin (6th century), this church adjacent to the Benedictine nunnery has only one aisle. Its unusual width is emphasized by three large arches which separate the area for the faithful from the area set apart for the nuns. A double-face altar was used by both sides. The church has been deconsecrated and now belongs to the city.

BIBLIOGRAPHY: Lorenzetti 1963, p. 366; Franzoi-Di Stefano 1976, pp. 467 ff.

135

Palazzo Donà dalle Rose at the Fondamente Nuove

1610-1611
Cannaregio 5038

Actv: Fondamente Nuove vaporetto stop

In the sobriety of the architectural lines, this building preserves the austere quality that Doge Leonardo Donà wished to impart to his residence, in open dispute with the spreading "Romanista" style and the growing taste for luxury. This is one of the few cases in which the original family still owns the building, keeping the furnishings and decorations intact.

BIBLIOGRAPHY: Bassi 1976, pp. 500 ff.; Concina 1989, pp. 121 ff.

136

Palazzo Pisani near Santo Stefano

1614-1615
Bartolomeo Monopola
San Marco 3395, Campiello Pisani

Actv: San Samuele or Accademia vaporetto stop

This is one of the most monumental palazzi in Venice, and was for the most part completed in the 18th century by Frigimelica. The façade overlooking the Campo is very large, and has superimposed Serlian motif windows, and pairs of windows with headed round arches. On the interior, there are two courtyards with superimposed loggias. Ever since 1897, the Conservatory has been located here.

BIBLIOGRAPHY: Bassi 1976, p. 360; Masobello-Tarlà 1976

137
Church of the Angelo Raffaele
1618-1639
Francesco Contin
Dorsoduro, Fondamenta dell'Angelo Raffaele
Actv: San Basilio vaporetto stop

This large church stands on the site of one of the oldest churches in Venice (7th century). Its clear tendency toward verticality is quite noteworthy, and can be detected in the 18th-century façade as well as in the interior with a Greek-cross plan and three aisles. The center is covered by a large cross-vault, held up by sizable pillars.

BIBLIOGRAPHY: *Franzoi-Di Stefano 1976, pp. 185 ff.*

138
Palazzo Treves de Bonfili
completed in 1632
Bartolomeo Monopola
San Marco 2156, Corte Barozzi
Actv: San Marco vaporetto stop

Although the palazzo is truly immense, the wing meant to be perpendicular to the Grand Canal was never built; the plan is thus two-, and not three-part. The façade that emerges as the most important is the one overlooking the Rio side – it is an exceptionally lengthy façade. The interiors, decorated in the early 19th century, are particularly worthy of note.

BIBLIOGRAPHY: *Bassi 1976, pp. 82 ff.*

139
Palazzo Albrizzi near San Cassian
circa 1600 and 1648-1692
San Polo 1490, Campiello Albrizzi
Actv: San Silvestro vaporetto stop

Built in a number of phases between the 16th and 17th centuries, the imposing bulk of this palazzo overlooks the Rio on two sides; the elevations are of some interest, certainly, and with their superimposed Serlian motif windows they are eloquent of a long-established manner. But of particular interest here are the interiors, among the most spectacular in Venice, decorated with white and gold stucco, frescoes, and medallions.

BIBLIOGRAPHY: *Bassi 1976, pp. 324 ff.*

140
Church of Santa Maria della Salute
1631-1681
Baldassare Longhena
Dorsoduro, Campo della Salute
Actv: Salute vaporetto stop

This church was built as a sign of thanksgiving after the plague of 1630; a dominant feature in the Venetian landscape, it was to become the setting for the termination of the annual votive pro-

cession. It marked the debut of the young Longhena, whose circular-plan design was chosen by the Venetian Senate out of eleven competing plans. The central plan, with a continuous deambulatory, is borrowed from proto-Christian and Byzantine examples. The plan is similar to that of the Redentore, but the architect here adds a presbytery comprising two semicircular apses. Particularly noteworthy is, in the central part, the vertical sequence of volumes that marks the transition from the lower, octagonal shape to the round dome.

BIBLIOGRAPHY: Muraro 1973; Howard 1980, p. 178; Biadene 1982, p. 102; Vio 1986

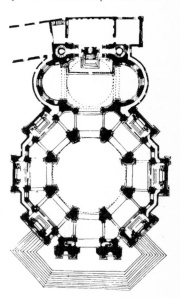

141
Church of Santa Maria del Pianto
1647-1659
Castello, Campo delle Cappuccine
Actv: Ospedale vaporetto stop

With a central plan and an octagonal shape, this Capuchin nunnery presents certain similarities to the church of the Salute; hence the attribution by some to Longhena (while others opt for Francesco Contin instead). The façade is of the simplified sort, with a curvilinear fronton that must have hinted at a dome that was however never built.

BIBLIOGRAPHY: Bassi 1962, pp. 70 ff.

142

Palazzo Giustinian-Lolin near San Vidal
1623-1625
Baldassare Longhena
San Marco 2893, Calle Giustinian
Actv: San Samuele or Accademia vaporetto stop

The model, established by Longhena in his youth, is heavily influenced by Scamozzi; in its cool elegance, the façade borrows architectural motifs, such as the centered and elongated windows, from Palazzo Contarini (see entry no. 131) which stands pratically opposite on the Grand Canal. Worthy of note are the interiors, where the Ugo and Olga Levi Foundation now has its offices.
BIBLIOGRAPHY: *Bassi 1976, p. 104; Biadene 1982, p. 60*

143

Palazzo Widmann-Rezzonico near San Cancian
completed in 1630
Baldassare Longhena
Cannaregio 5403, Fondamenta Widmann
Actv: Ca' d'Oro or Rialto vaporetto stop

This building, too, was designed by Longhena in his earliest phase. In particular in the elevation overlooking the Rio of San Cancian we find elements borrowed by Serlio and from Sansovino, as well as from Longhena's master, Scamozzi. This sort of neo-16th-century compendium becomes extremely common in civil architecture of the mid-17th century.
BIBLIOGRAPHY: *Bassi 1976, pp. 261; Biadene 1982, p. 62*

144

Library at San Giorgio Maggiore
1641-1671
Baldassare Longhena
Island of San Giorgio
Actv: San Giorgio vaporetto stop

Longhena was summoned after the fire that destroyed the library by Michelozzo. He worked only, in the large open space, on the large windows overlooking the courtyard and the bizarre wooden shelving (later diligently restored). In 1643, he also designed the multi-flight ceremonial staircase which provides access to the library (see entries nos. 113, 114).
BIBLIOGRAPHY: *Bassi 1962, pp. 112 ff.; Biadene 1982, pp. 130 ff.*

145

Former Church of Santa Giustina

circa 1640
Baldassare Longhena
Castello, Campo Santa Giustina
Actv: Celestia vaporetto stop

This church, now deconsecrated, is part of the Liceo Scientifico Giambattista Benedetti, a high school; it was wrapped up with the commemoration of the Battle of Lepanto (which took place on Saint Justine's Day). Longhena designed the façade in celebrative forms, with giant-order Corinthian columns, designed to support a curvilinear fronton which was never built however.

BIBLIOGRAPHY: *Bassi 1962, pp. 110*

146

Scuola Grande of the Carmini

1627-1663, and 1668-1670
Baldassare Longhena
Dorsoduro, Campo Santa Margherita
Actv: Ca' Rezzonico o San Basilio vaporetto stop

In this building, known principally for the paintings by G.B. Tiepolo, Longhena developed a façade with two orders of paired half-columns, set on high plinths; the side elevation has a rusticated basement and two portals with tympanums. Decorated lavishly, the interior is rectangular in shape, and is split up into two parts on each floor.

BIBLIOGRAPHY: *Bassi 1962, pp. 154 ff.; Pignatti 1981, pp. 201 ff.*

147

Palazzo da Lezze near the Misericordia

1650-1660
Baldassare Longhena
Cannaregio 3598, Fondamenta della Misericordia
Actv: San Marcuola o Ca' d'Oro vaporetto stop

In the extensive elevation along the Rio there appear, in expanded form, all the features that typify the 17th-century maner; in the lateral façade, alongside the Scuola of the Misericordia, the same features appear in a contracted form. Faced with a complex plan, Longhena thus demonstrates an almost virtuosic mastery of the language.

BIBLIOGRAPHY: *Bassi 1976, p. 282; Biadene 1982, p. 64*

148

Ca' Pesaro
1652-1682, 1703-1710
Baldassare Longhena and Antonio Gaspari
Santa Croce 2076, Fondamenta Pesaro
Actv: San Stae vaporetto stop

The traditional type plan of this huge palazzo was constrained by the necessity of assembling three different buildings into one, as we can see from the design still at the Correr Museum. The elevations seem to have been more successful; the tripartite scheme, influenced by the work of Sansovino, were refined in line with a more emphatic predilection for the plastic. The columns on the *piano nobile* are separated from the façade, the ashlars of the basement are cut to the shape of diamonds. At Longhena's death (1682), the giant construction had risen to the first floor (while the volumetric plan had extended to the front overlooking the interior courtyard) and it was completed by Gaspari twenty years later. Since 1923, this building has housed the Museum of Contemporary Art and the Oriental Museum.
BIBLIOGRAPHY: *Bassi 1976, p. 174; Biadene 1982, p. 70*

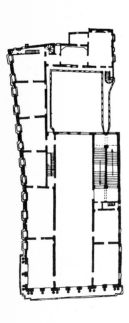

149

Ospedaletto and Church of Santa Maria dei Derelitti
1667-1674
Giuseppe Sardi and Baldassare Longhena
Castello 6690, Barbaria delle Tole
Actv: Ospedale vaporetto stop

Founded in 1527, construction on this version of the Ospedaletto was begun in the 18th century by Giuseppe Sardi (all that remains of his project is the oval staircase) and was completed by Longhena. He also built the adjacent church, conceived as a rectangular hall with three altars on each side; the façade is heavy with a double order of sculptural and architectural elements.
BIBLIOGRAPHY: *Pilo 1985; Aikema-Meijers 1989, p. 149*

150

Ca' Rezzonico

1667-1682 and 1750-1758
Baldassare Longhena and Giorgio Massari
Dorsoduro 1336, Fondamenta Rezzonico
Actv: Ca' Rezzonico vaporetto stop

Aside from the size and the other stylistic similarities, there are a great many analogies that link this palazzo – originally built for the Priuli-Bon family – with Ca' Pesaro. In particular, we should mention the large plan and the elongated form which turns its short side to the Grand Canal. In both cases, Longhena died when the huge buildings had reached their first floor. This led to the introduction of a second architect. Giorgio Massari did not stop at simply completing the building: he invented a ballroom which concludes the plan on the west and gives the decorations and the nature of the interiors an 18th-century air. It is no accident that the Museum of 18th-Century Venice has been located here since 1935.

BIBLIOGRAPHY: *Lorenzetti 1936; Bassi 1976, pp. 114 ff.; Biadene 1982, pp. 90 ff.*

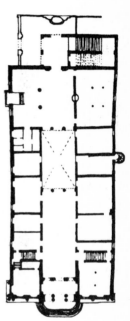

151

Patriarchal Seminary

1669-1670
Baldassare Longhena
Dorsoduro 1, Punta della Salute
* *Salute vaporetto stop*

The building was constructed on behalf of the Somaschi fathers, with a quadrilateral shape that derived from an existing cloister of the monastery of the Trinità. In Venice, after the expulsion of the Jesuits, the Somaschi performed the role of educators. After the suppression of the convent (1810), the Patriarchal Seminary – previously on Murano – was set up here.

BIBLIOGRAPHY: *Bassi 1962, pp. 156 ff.*

152
Scuola of San Nicolò and Collegio Flangini
1678-1680
Baldassare Longhena
Castello 3412, Rio dei Greci
Actv: San Zaccaria vaporetto stop

Around the church of San Giorgio (see entry no. 88), there accumulated a complex of buildings belonging to the Greek community. Set within a wall, which was itself a careful piece of design, this small and elegant Scuola took shape alongside Palazzo Flangini, with a harmonious rusticated front with sharply defined framed surfaces. Today it houses several Greek cultural institutions.
BIBLIOGRAPHY: *Bassi* 1962, p. 168; *Concina* 1989, p. 80

153
Palazzo Battaglia near San Stae
circa 1650
Santa Croce 1783, Calle del Megio
Actv: San Stae vaporetto stop

The traditional features of the elevation appear deformed here, arranged according to a different order: the *piano nobile* is remarkably tall, and is emphasized above all by broken pediments, while the upper floors appear to be understated. Behind this design, once senses an expert and skillful hand, such as that of a mature Longhena.
BIBLIOGRAPHY: *Bassi* 1976, pp. 194 ff.

154
Palazzo Flangini near San Geremia
1660-1680
Cannaregio 250, Campiello Flangini
Actv: Stazione vaporetto stop

Here too one senses the self-assured style of Longhena; the regular portions of the façade overlooking the Grand Canal suggest analogies with Ca' Pesaro and Ca' Rezzonico. No lateral wing was built, and so the plan and the elevation of the composition is asymmetrical; despite that, the building appears balanced.
BIBLIOGRAPHY: *Bassi* 1976, pp. 220 ff.

155

Palazzo Moro-Lin near San Samuele
circa 1670
Sebastiano Mazzoni
San Marco 3242, Calle Morolin
Actv: San Samuele vaporetto stop

Designed by a Tuscan painter for a client who was also a painter, this building *in volta de Canal* is referred to as the palazzo with thirteen windows. Entirely rusticated, the elevation overlooking the water appears nicely punctuated throughout by a sequence of windows, alternating with pilaster strips. In 1703, a story was added, in a fairly brutal manner.
BIBLIOGRAPHY: Bassi 1976, pp. 480 ff.

156

Scuola Ponentina at the Ghetto Vecchio
completed around 1660
Cannaregio 1149, Calle del Ghetto Vecchio
Actv: Ponte delle Guglie vaporetto stop

This synagogue, which is also known as the Scuola Spagnola, or Spanish School, has often been attributed to Longhena; actually, as Concina states, this is "the first thoroughly architectural structure built in the Ghetto's history." If the interior is, typically, built as a hall with a *matroneum*, the exterior is punctuated by four large windows set above the portal.
BIBLIOGRAPHY: Concina 1991, pp. 124 ff.

157

Scuola Levantina at the Ghetto Vecchio
1638-1700
Cannaregio 1228, Calle del Ghetto Vecchio
Actv: Ponte delle Guglie vaporetto stop

This synagogue, belonging to the Ashkenazi, accentuates characteristics that were already present in the Scuola Spagnola. There are not only introverted features here as seen in the Scuola has an elevation marked by framed surfaces and by rounded arches in carved stone. On the interior, the *tevà*, or wooden canopied altar with spiral columns, stands out.
BIBLIOGRAPHY: Concina 1991, pp. 133 ff.

158

Scuola Grande of San Teodoro
1579-1613 and 1649-1655
Tommaso Contin and Giuseppe Sardi
San Marco 4811, Campo San Salvador
Actv: Rialto vaporetto stop

The twin façades of San Salvador and the Scuola Grande dominate the Campo: with double orders, crowned by tympanums and acroteria, both façades were built by Sardi, between 1649 and 1663, through the generous bequest left by the merchant Jacopo Galli. The Scuola thus appears to have been concluded after a difficult and complex series of events that found resolution only after 1608.
BIBLIOGRAPHY: *Bassi 1962, pp. 73, 186 ff.*

159

Church of the Scalzi
1660-89
Baldassare Longhena and Giuseppe Sardi
Cannaregio, Fondamenta della Stazione
Actv: Stazione vaporetto stop

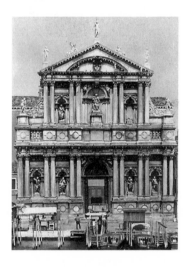

In comparison with the Ospedaletto, here the roles are reversed. The plan was conceived by Longhena with one aisle and side chapels; to this, after 1672, Sardi added an elaborate front, with a double order of paired columns that define the spaces for the niches. The remarkably lavish ornamentation does nothing to undercut the overall harmony of the composition.
BIBLIOGRAPHY: *Bassi 1962, p. 190; Franzoi-Di Stefano 1976, pp. 98 ff.*

160

Church of Santa Maria del Giglio
1678-1783
Giuseppe Sardi
San Marco, Campo Santa Maria del Giglio
Actv: Santa Maria del Giglio vaporetto stop

Even richer and more elaborate in this façade is the double-order previously used by Sardi in the Church of the Scalzi. In this case, we are looking at a church rebuilt at the expense, and to the glory of, the Barbaro family; the family is depicted in the four statues in niches and references to the family are made in the curious reliefs of fortified cities in the lower stylobate.
BIBLIOGRAPHY: *Bassi 1962, pp. 196 ff.; Franzoi-Di Stefano 1976, pp. 326 ff.*

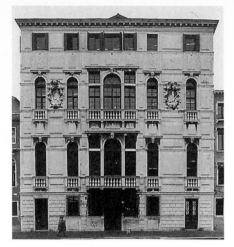

161

Palazzo Savorgnan near San Geremia

circa 1680
Giuseppe Sardi
Cannaregio 349, Fondamenta Savorgnan
Actv: Ponte delle Guglie vaporetto stop

In the elevation overlooking the Canal of Cannaregio, we find all of the features that typify 17th-century civil architecture (rustication, framed surfaces, centered windows with headed round arch) as codified in the work of Longhena. The interiors, too, with sculptural decorations, and polychrome or *rosso di Verona* marble, seem to correspond to the taste and expectations of the time.

BIBLIOGRAPHY: *Bassi 1976, pp. 293 ff.*

162

Church of Santa Croce degli Armeni

1675-1682
San Marco, Calle degli Armeni
Actv: San Marco or San Zaccaria vaporetto stop

Near San Zulian, in an area inhabited by the Armenian community, stands this small church of the Mechitarist fathers. Completely inwardly oriented, it comprises a cube atop which sits a hemispheric dome. This work is therefore a product of the Neo-Byzantine tradition, and many attribute it to Giuseppe Sardi.

BIBLIOGRAPHY: *Bassi 1962, pp. 195 ff.; Franzoi-Di Stefano 1976, p. 362*

163

Dogana da Mar

1677-1678
Giuseppe Benoni
Dorsoduro, Punta della Salute
Actv: Salute vaporetto stop

Of the many designs presented (first by Longhena, and later by Sardi and Cominelli), the plan by the hydraulic engineer Benoni was chosen. This is a strange building, which is called upon to face the basin of Saint Mark's. The corner tower, with its gold ball, constitutes the culmination of the plan, horizontally and vertically, and crowns a composition rich in architectural features.

BIBLIOGRAPHY: *Bassi 1962, pp. 158 ff.*

164
Bridge of the Tre Archi
1688
Andrea Tirali
Cannaregio, Canale di Cannaregio
Actv: Tre Archi vaporetto stop

This was the first project by Tirali, who had just been named deputy supervisor (*viceproto*) of the Magistratura alla Acque. The bridge is based on a concept taken from the techniques of the ancients. With its raised central arch, it is reminiscent of the model presented by Scamozzi, a hundred years previous, for the reconstruction of Rialto.
BIBLIOGRAPHY: Bassi 1962, p. 270

165
Church of San Moisè
begun in 1668
Alessandro Tremignon
San Marco, Campo San Moisè
Actv: San Marco vaporetto stop

This church was renovated over the course of the 17th century, based on the original medieval building. A considerable bequest by the Fini family made it possible to build a new façade, which Tremignon conceived in cheerfully exuberant forms. The tripartite scheme of post-Palladian churches is here thrown into confusion by decorative excess.
BIBLIOGRAPHY: Bassi 1962, pp. 233 ff.; Franzoi-Di Stefano 1976, pp. 318 ff.

166
Palazzo Fini near San Moisè
circa 1688
Alessandro Tremignon
San Marco 2322, Calle Minotto
Actv: San Marco vaporetto stop

This building was erected for the Greek Flangini family, and subsequent to 1688 was rebuilt by the Fini family architect. It has structures and features of a conventional type, such as the polyforate windows with balusters and in double series, and none of the exuberance of San Moisè. Now it is the headquarters of the Council of the Region of Venetia.
BIBLIOGRAPHY: Bassi 1976, pp. 86 ff.

167

Palazzo Michiel delle Colonne
completed in 1697
Antonio Gaspari
Cannaregio 4314, Calle del Duca
Actv: Ca' d'Oro vaporetto stop

The façade overlooking the Grand Canal reveals the history of this palazzo modified in its appearance by Gaspari. The origin of its name ("delle Colonne") is the high (disproportionately so) colonnade on the ground floor which reveals the Veneto-Byzantine structure of the building. In the 18th century it became the home of the Gonzaga family.
BIBLIOGRAPHY: *Bassi 1962, p. 248*

168

Palazzo Giustinian at Murano
1689-1700
Antonio Gaspari
Murano, Fondamenta Giustinian
Actv: Museo vaporetto stop

This palazzo, built in the 14th century, was transformed by Gaspari into something with forms typical of the late 17th century, though simplified. In 1707, when the patriarchal headquarters were moved from Torcello to Murano, this building became the residence of the bishop of Torcello (and so it remained until 1805). Since 1861 the Glass Museum has been located here.
BIBLIOGRAPHY: *Bassi 1962, p. 248; Lorenzetti 1963, pp. 808 ff.*

169

Palazzo Zenobio near the Carmini
1689-1700
Antonio Gaspari
Dorsoduro 2593-97, Fondamenta del Soccorso
Actv: Ca' Rezzonico vaporetto stop

On the side overlooking the Rio, the lengthy elevation is enlivened at the center by a Roman-style curvilinear fronton; in the façade's rather monotonous development, it actually conceals a complex plan, in the shape of a large "C," which opens in the rear toward a handsome, Italian garden. Owned by the Mechitarist fathers, this palazzo houses the Collegio Armeno.
BIBLIOGRAPHY: *Bassi 1976, pp. 348 ff.*

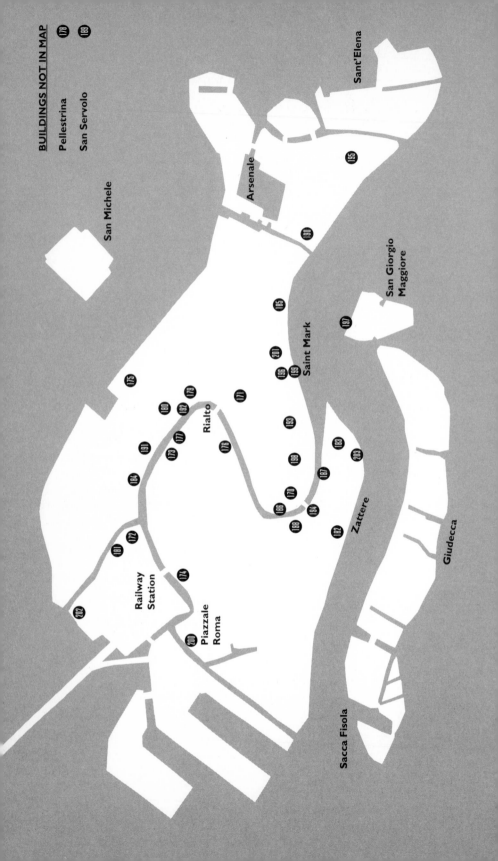

San Michele

Arsenale

Sant'Elena

175

180
192
179

191
173

184

172
181

202

Railway
Station

174

200

Piazzale
Roma

Rialto

177

176

171

105

201

196
199

Saint Mark

193

198

186

170

194

188

182

Zattere

185

187

203

195

190

197

San Giorgio
Maggiore

Giudecca

Sacca Fisola

Eighteenth-Century and Neo-Classical Venice

The music of Vivaldi, the comedies of Goldoni, the paintings of Guardi and Canaletto, the last glimmers of a world on its way to final dissolution. It is not a great century, on the other hand, for Venetian architecture, unless we are to judge it purely in terms of size and luxury. In that case, we would have to say that the enormous palazzi (more or less completed) along the Grand Canal were spectacular achievements.

No one architect stands out from the others; Tirali and Massari come first, followed by Visentini, Temanza, and Scalfarotto, sharing in particular their reliance on Palladian models. Many 18th-century churches imitate the façade of San Giorgio; noteworthy and original is the plan of the interior of the Pietà, perhaps the single most significant piece of architecture from this period.

It is only in the last few years of the century that the figure of Selva emerges, debuting with his design for the La Fenice theater. After the fall of the Republic, he was to become the architect of the great Napoleonic projects: the royal palace and gardens at San Marco, but also new public structures such as the Quadreria (art gallery), the city hospital, the state archives, all of which were installed in convents wrested from the church. In this phase (referred to as Neo-Classical), the architect tended to select and emphasize only a few elements from the language of the ancients. In the age of the Restoration, too, the concept of public building was to be expressed with a simplified classicism.

170

Former Church of San Vidal
1696-1700 and 1734-1737
Antonio Gaspari and Andrea Tirali
San Marco, Campo Santo Stefano
Actv: San Samuele or Accademia vaporetto stop

With funding from the bequest of the Doge Contarini, the medieval structure was transformed by Gaspari into a single-nave building. The façade was later built according to a Neo-Palladian design by Tirali, quite similar to that of San Francesco della Vigna. No longer a place of worship, the building now houses temporary exhibitions.
BIBLIOGRAPHY: *Bassi 1962, pp. 284 ff.; Franzoi-Di Stefano 1976, pp. 337 ff.*

171

Church of Santa Maria della Fava
1705-15 e 1750-53
Antonio Gaspari and Giorgio Massari
Castello, Campo della Fava
Actv: Rialto vaporetto stop

Here, Gaspari was unsuccessful in carrying to completion a series of plans, clearly influenced by the work of Borromini, marked by curvilinear and superimposed geometric motifs; although it was not the original plan, the renovation of the interior (a hall with rounded corners) is not completely devoid of elegance, in part due to the later work done by Massari, architect of the presbytery and the ceiling.
BIBLIOGRAPHY: *Bassi 1962; Franzoi-Di Stefano 1976*

172

Palazzo Labia
around 1700
Alessandro Tremignon and Andrea Cominelli
Cannaregio 334, Campo San Geremia
Actv: Stazione vaporetto stop

The chronology of this great palazzo is not known. The style of the interiors, well-known for their spectacular decorations and frescoes, belongs to that period. All of the façades are similar to the models of Longhena; the one overlooking the Campo is by Tremignon, while those on the water are by Cominelli. This is the regional headquarters of RAI state television and radio.
BIBLIOGRAPHY: *Bassi 1976, pp. 204 ff.; Martinelli-Pedrocco-Pignatti 1982*

173

Church of San Stae

1678-1700 and 1709-1710
Giovanni Grassi and Domenico Rossi
Santa Croce, Campo San Stae
Actv: San Stae vaporetto stop

The interior is by Grassi; it has a single aisle and side chapels, and contains paintings by the leading artists of the 18th century. Of the twelve designs proposed for the façade, Rossi's was chosen, with giant-order Corinthian columns, set on high plinths. There are also statues in the niches and atop the tympanum. This would appear to be a transitional design, coming between the Baroque *a la* Sardi and the Neo-Palladian style.
BIBLIOGRAPHY: *Tramontin 1961; Franzoi-Di Stefano 1976*

174

Church of San Simon Piccolo

1718-1738
Giovanni Antonio Scalfarotto
Santa Croce, Fondamenta San Simon Piccolo
Actv: Stazione vaporetto stop

This curious building is modelled in the image of the Pantheon; here too a pronaos, with Corinthian columns, stands before a central-plan building in which the dome appears, however, out of proportion to the drum. It is said, in this connection, that the Proto Scalfarotto meant to build a counterpart to the Salute, set on the far end of the Grand Canal.
BIBLIOGRAPHY: *Bassi 1962, pp. 335 ff.; Franzoi-Di Stefano 1976, pp. 77 ff.*

175

Church of the Gesuiti

1715-1728
Domenico Rossi
Cannaregio, Campo dei Gesuiti
Actv: Fondamente Nuove vaporetto stop

Once they were allowed to return to Venice (1657), the Jesuits purchased the convent of the Crosecheri, but they were unable to rebuild its medieval church until much later. The layout is lengthwise, with deep lateral chapels and a central dome; the façade, too, perhaps built in collaboration with Giovanni Battista Fattoretto, echoes the Jesuit prototype.
BIBLIOGRAPHY: *Bassi 1962, pp. 218 ff.; Franzoi-Di Stefano 1976, pp. 150 ff.*

176
Palazzo Maffetti-Tiepolo
1712
Domenico Rossi
San Polo 1957, Campo San Polo
Actv: San Tomà or San Silvestro vaporetto stop

The façade overlooking the Campo in particular clearly betrays the influence of the models developed by Longhena and Sardi; typical of Rossi's work, as Elena Bassi has noted, is the treatment of the keystones and the modillions. This is particularly true of the elements that surround the portal, resolved like full-fledged sculptures.

BIBLIOGRAPHY: *Bassi 1976, pp. 338 ff.*

177
Ca' Corner della Regina
1724-1727
Domenico Rossi
Santa Croce 2214, Calle Corner
Actv: San Stae vaporetto stop

Like the nearby Ca' Pesaro, this palazzo too presents an elongated plan; Rossi resolved it according to a symmetrical scheme, despite the irregular shape of the area. On the short side, overlooking the Grand Canal, the customary repertory of stylistic elements reappears, composed with their proportions vertically deformed.

BIBLIOGRAPHY: *Bassi 1976, pp. 166 ff.*

178
Church of Santa Maria del Soccorso (or San Vito)
1723
Andrea Tirali
Pellestrina
Actv: Pellestrina vaporetto stop

This small church made of Istrian stone was built by Tirali in the context of water fortifications (including the *murazzi*) which he built in the estuary, as Proto of the Magistratura alla Acque; this is an octagonal-plan building which appears, in its borrowing of Palladian motifs, thoroughly Neo-Classical.

BIBLIOGRAPHY: *Lorenzetti 1963, p. 835*

179
Scuola dell'Angelo Custode
circa 1730
Andrea Tirali
Cannaregio, Campo Santi Apostoli
Actv: Ca' d'Oro vaporetto stop

This building, which is now an Evangelical church, is the last Scuola built in Venice; the structure is traditional, with a lower and an upper hall, connected by a two-flight stairway. Along the four façades there are cornices punctuated only by the pediments above the windows.

BIBLIOGRAPHY: *Bassi* 1962, pp. 280 ff.

180
Palazzo Diedo near Santa Fosca
1710-1720
Andrea Tirali
Cannaregio 2386, Fondamenta Diedo
Actv: San Marcuola vaporetto stop

Surrounded by canals and low buildings, this palazzo has four façades and four entries, arranged around a cross-shaped atrium. The elevations have very little decoration: on the bare surface, interrupted only by framed surfaces and horizontal bands, the elongated, centered windows stand out. Today, this is an elementary school.

BIBLIOGRAPHY: *Bassi* 1976, pp. 450 ff.

181
Palazzo Priuli-Manfrin
circa 1735
Andrea Tirali
Cannaregio 423, Ponte delle Guglie
Actv: Stazione or San Marcuola vaporetto stop

In relation to this building by Tirali in his latest period, there are those who have alluded to modernist tendencies: the façade overlooking the canal has a sharply defined layout, in which the sequence of rectangular windows is punctuated only by framed surfaces. The plan is unusual, and is not tripartite, but organized around a small central courtyard.

BIBLIOGRAPHY: *Bassi* 1962, pp. 288 ff.

182

Church and Convent of Santa Maria del Rosario (or Gesuati)

1726-1736
Giorgio Massari
Dorsoduro, Zattere ai Gesuati
Actv: Zattere vaporetto stop

The tripartite façade with its tall Corinthian columns makes use of Palladian motifs, clearly visible as well in the plan (the choir with double apse and the side chapels). In the curvilinear formation of the interior, the exedra with colonnade behind the main altar stands out. The adjacent convent with a quadriporticus and an oval staircase probably dates from around 1750.
BIBLIOGRAPHY: *Bassi 1962; Franzoi-Di Stefano 1976*

183

Hospice of the Catecumeni

1727
Giorgio Massari
Dorsoduro 108, Rio Terà dei Catecumeni
Actv: Salute vaporetto stop

This building served for marshalling and housing Levantine prisoners, awaiting conversion. Massari renovated its layout according to the standard 16th- or 17th-century approach: two courtyards arranged on the sides of the church which faces outward, its elevations interrupting the monotony and stylistic poverty of the surrounding façades.
BIBLIOGRAPHY: *Aikema-Meijers 1989, pp. 215 ff.*

184

Church of San Marcuola

1728-1736
Giorgio Massari
Cannaregio, Campo San Marcuola
Actv: San Marcuola vaporetto stop

The first nucleus of the new church was the chapel of the main altar, rebuilt in the 17th century. Once Gaspari's designs were rejected, Massari was able to use the standard approach of a single aisle with side chapels with rounded corners. Of the façade, only the portal and four plinths were completed, hinting at a structure that might well have been similar to that of the Pietà.
BIBLIOGRAPHY: *Bassi 1962, pp. 306 ff.; Franzoi-Di Stefano 1976, pp. 117 ff.*

185
Church of the Pietà (or of the Visitazione)
1744-1760
Giorgio Massari
Castello, Riva degli Schiavoni
Actv: San Zaccaria vaporetto stop

This building, which dates from the 15th century, was known for the concerts given by the orchestras of girls from the hospice (*ospelaere*, the girls were called), directed by Vivaldi. Massari redesigned the church, and his customary motif of round forms in this case gave rise to a central plan (preceded by a vestibule as in Scamozzi's church. Acoustic requirements and references to illustrious examples (Roman Baroque, Sansovino's work on the Incurabili) led to an oval plan, harmoniously resolved in the façades. The frescoes by Tiepolo complete a remarkable artistic whole which has led some to speak of a masterpiece of 18th-century Venetian architecture. Massari's design for a hospital was not to be completed.

BIBLIOGRAPHY: *Franzoi-Di Stefano 1976, pp. 481 ff.; Aikema-Meijers 1989, pp. 197 ff.*

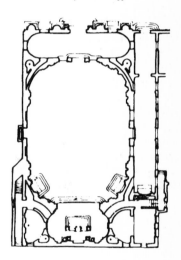

186
Palazzo Grassi
1748-1772
Giorgio Massari
San Marco 3231, Campo San Samuele
Actv: San Samuele vaporetto stop

The last, anachronistic patrician palazzo, built to a grandiose scale on the banks of the Grand Canal; it is trapezoidal in shape, and is arranged around a monumental colonnaded courtyard, which also features a three-flight staircase. Owned by the IFI-FIAT group, it is the headquarters of the Palazzo Grassi Foundation, and is currently used to hold art exhibitions of international importance.

BIBLIOGRAPHY: *Bassi 1962, pp. 324 ff.; Romanelli-Pavanello 1986.*

107

187

**Palazzo Venier dei Leoni
(Peggy Guggenheim Foundation)**
1749
Lorenzo Boschetti
Dorsoduro 701, Calle San Cristoforo
Actv: Accademia or Salute vaporetto stop

Constructed at the same time as Palazzo Grassi, this building was intended to equal its size and monumental appearance. In reality, only the basement of white Istrian stone, facing the Grand Canal, was completed at the time. Became the residence of Peggy Guggenheim, who collected the works of the leading artists of the 20th century here, it is now a museum bearing her name.
BIBLIOGRAPHY: *Bassi 1962, p. 342*

188

Church of San Barnaba
1749-1776
Lorenzo Boschetti
Dorsoduro, Campo San Barnaba
Actv: Ca' Rezzonico vaporetto stop

The façade, made entirely of Istrian stone with a single order of Corinthian columns, is a faithful copy of the model developed by the Jesuits. In the single-aisle interior we find elements taken from the architecture of Massari, such as the half-columns on high plinths and a clear predilection for polychrome juxtapositions.
BIBLIOGRAPHY: *Franzoi-Di Stefano 1976, pp. 198 ff.*

189

Church and Hospital of San Servolo
1734-1759
Tomaso Temanza and Giovanni Antonio Scalfarotto
Island of San Servolo
Actv: San Servolo vaporetto stop

Over the course of the 18th-century, on the site of a previous Benedictine complex, there grew up a hospital complex intended for the mentally ill (and so it remained until 1975, with the deinstitutionalization of the insane in Italy). The small church was transformed by Temanza in 1749, while the hospital is by Scalfarotto, presumably in the same years.
BIBLIOGRAPHY: *Lorenzetti 1963, pp. 797 ff.*

190

Church of San Biagio
1749-1754
Filippo Rossi
Castello, Riva San Biagio
Actv: Arsenale vaporetto stop

Once an orthodox church, this building was transformed into its curious modern form by the Proto Sopra le Fabbriche dell'Arsenale, or the Magistrate in Charge of Building at the Arsenale. It was officially made the church of the Venetian Navy in 1818, and the monument to Angelo Emo, the last admiral and reformer of the Venetian fleet, was moved there at that time.

BIBLIOGRAPHY: *Franzoi-Di Stefano 1976, pp. 500 ff.*

191

Church of the Maddalena
circa 1760
Tomaso Temanza
Cannaregio, Campo della Maddalena
Actv: San Marcuola vaporetto stop

This is a central-plan building, which Temanza set upon a hexagonally shaped perimeter. On the exterior, it appears – in emulation of the Pantheon – as an assemblage of a squat dome and a drum, preceded by a pronaos (in this case, jointed to the volume and sustained by pairs of Ionic columns).

BIBLIOGRAPHY: *Franzoi-Di Stefano 1976, pp. 120 ff.*

192

Palazzetto Mangilli-Valmarana
1740-1751
Antonio Visentini
Cannaregio 4392, Rio dei Santi Apostoli
Actv: Ca' d'Oro vaporetto stop

The central cornice marks the line of the eaves of the original building; which is not inelegant, if considered in that light. It was built by Visentini for the proconsul Smith, a well known collector and a patron of the arts. After 1784 Giannantonio Selva designed the added, higher floors, and in so doing redesigned the interior decoration of the entire building.

BIBLIOGRAPHY: *Bassi 1962, pp. 362 ff.; Bassi 1976, pp. 9 ff.*

193

La Fenice Theater
1790-1792
Giannantonio Selva
San Marco 1965, Campo San Fantin
Actv: Santa Maria del Giglio or San Marco vaporetto stop
The young Selva, surprisingly, won the competition to build the great theater. Selva revealed a surprising ability to insert the complex array of functions required for the theater into a difficult area; his contemporaries were impressed by the great hall of the theater, shaped like a horse-shoe as was common at the time, and decorated with great elegance. On a completely different scale, but still quite effective, was the Sala Apollinea, named for the philharmonic orchestra that played there until 1860. The main façade, on Campo San Fantin, appears understated, despite the entry colonnade. In 1836, the building was destroyed by fire. The Meduna brothers, students of Selva, managed to rebuild it staying quite faithful to the original.
BIBLIOGRAPHY: *Mangini 1974, pp. 165 ff.; Brusatin-Pavanello 1987; Romanelli 1988, pp. 297 ff.*

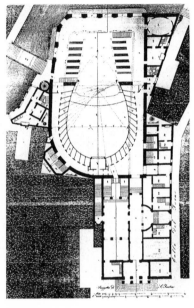

194

Galleria and Accademia delle Belle Arti
1807-1811
Giannantonio Selva
Dorsoduro 1050, Campo della Carità
Actv: Accademia vaporetto stop
This institution dates from 1750, but it was not until the Napoleonic suppressions that it found its current location, in the Lateran convent, the church and the Scuola della Carità (see entries nos. 46, 111). Francesco Lazzari created a new entry, transforming the front while a new loggia connects it to the Palladian wing and to the former church, split into two rooms one atop the other.
BIBLIOGRAPHY: *Bassi 1978; Romanelli 1978/a, pp. 238 ff.; Biadene 1985/a*

195

Napoleonic Gardens
1810
Giannantonio Selva
Castello, Via Garibaldi
Actv: Giardini vaporetto stop

The project formed part of the plan of embellishment developed by the Commission of Ornaments in 1807. Perpendicular to the new Via Eugenia (now Via Garibaldi), the green area was obtained by demolishing buildings that were mostly religious structures. The park was designed as a tree-lined walkway, enclosing a series of small monuments.
BIBLIOGRAPHY: *Romanelli 1977*, pp. 50 ff.; *Romanelli 1978/b*, pp. 197 ff.

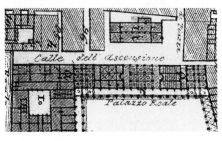

196

Napoleonic Wing
1810-1815
Giovanni Antonio Antolini, Giuseppe Maria Soli, and Lorenzo Santi
San Marco 76-79, Saint Mark's Square
Actv: San Marco vaporetto stop

This structure was linked to the creation of an access stairway and a ballroom for the Royal Palace. It closes the short side of the piazza to the side of the Procuratie Vecchie, whence it takes its decorative version; the opposite elevation, at the opening of the square, is more in line with the style of the period. In order to build it, the church of San Geminiano by Sansovino was demolished.
BIBLIOGRAPHY: *Romanelli 1977*, p. 77; *Biadene 1985/b*

197

Dockyards of the Free Port
1810-1815
Giuseppe Mezzani, R. Venturelli
Island of San Giorgio
Actv: San Giorgio vaporetto stop

After the suppression of the Benedictine convent, in 1806 the entire island was made a free zone. At that point, a structural backdrop, between the convent and the new landing area, was developed, to be used as docks. Facing it is the darsena, with a breakwater and two small light-towers, set at either end, and made entirely of blocks of Istrian stone.
BIBLIOGRAPHY: *Romanelli 1977*, pp. 102 ff.

198

Church of San Maurizio
1806-1828
Giannantonio Selva and Antonio Diedo
San Marco, Campo San Maurizio
Actv: Santa Maria del Giglio vaporetto stop

The existing structure was modified until it took on the shape of a Greek cross; the scheme is Codussian in style with a central dome and four barrel-vaulted arms. Their similarity made it possible to reproduce the main façade, overlooking the Campo, according to simple classical motifs.
BIBLIOGRAPHY: *Franzoi-Di Stefano 1976, pp. 329 ff.*

199

Coffee House near the Royal Gardens
1815-1817
Lorenzo Santi
San Marco, Molo, or Saint Mark's Wharf
Actv: San Marco vaporetto stop

Designed during the Napoleonic period, this small and graceful building must have been part of the royal landholdings created in 1806 with the demolition of the granaries; aulic architecture on a Lilliputian scale, the coffee house was built at the beginning of the Restoration.
BIBLIOGRAPHY: *Romanelli 1977, pp. 185 ff.; Romanelli 1988, pp. 169 ff.*

200

Church of the Nome di Gesù
1815-1834
Giannantonio Selva and Antonio Diedo
Santa Croce, Fondamenta Santa Chiara
Actv: Piazzale Roma vaporetto stop

In this small and harmonious church we can clearly see the archeological style, of English derivation. On the interior, it is worth noting the use of the barrel vault arranged transversally across the presbytery and divided by two Ionic columns.
BIBLIOGRAPHY: *Franzoi-Di Stefano 1976, pp. 90 ff.; Romanelli 1978/b, pp. 229 ff.*

201

Patriarch's Palace
1836-1850
Lorenzo Santi
San Marco 318, Piazzetta dei Leoncini
Actv: San Zaccaria vaporetto stop

The purpose of this building was two-fold – to give the patriarch a new home near Saint Mark's, which had recently been made a cathedral, and to confer a decorous appearance on the Piazzetta, where the north side of the basilica and the Doge's Palace converge. Of the twenty models proposed, the most clearly Neo-Classical one – especially in its façade – was chosen.
BIBLIOGRAPHY: Romanelli 1977, pp. 189 ff.

202

General Slaughterhouse near San Giobbe
1841-1843
Giuseppe Salvadori
Cannaregio, Fondamenta San Giobbe
Actv: Tre Archi vaporetto stop

The project dates back to 1834; it was drawn up by the head of the City Technical Board, in collaboration with Giovanni Battista Meduna. The complex comprises a series of low buildings arranged in herring-bone fashion, joined by a continuous element – a decorous Neo-Classic elevation facing the lagoon, visible even from a great distance.
BIBLIOGRAPHY: Romanelli 1978/a, pp. 234 ff.; Mazzotta 1990/a

203

Salt Warehouse
circa 1830
Giovanni Alvise Pigazzi
Dorsoduro, Zattere ai Saloni
Actv: Salute vaporetto stop

The long front overlooking the Canal of Giudecca is punctuated by a regular sequence of openings, each of which corresponds to a *salone* perpendicular to the front. This structure, rebuilt and redecorated in conformity to a decorous Neo-Classical standard, stands on a complex of 15th-century buildings.
BIBLIOGRAPHY: Mazzotta 1990/b

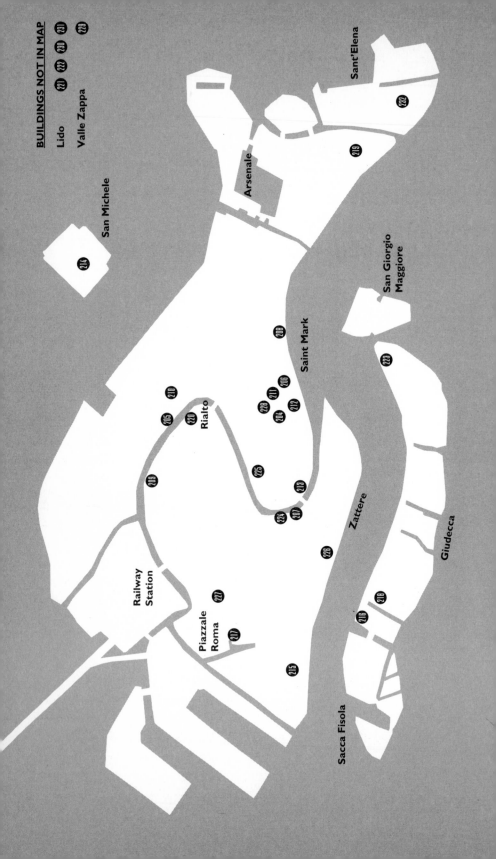

BUILDINGS NOT IN MAP

Lido 221 222 230 231

Valle Zappa 229

San Michele

Arsenale

Sant'Elena

Saint Mark

San Giorgio
Maggiore

Rialto

Railway
Station

Piazzale
Roma

Zattere

Giudecca

Sacca Fisola

214

232

219

223

208

210

205 220

211 206

228 204 212

225

209

213

224 207

226

221

217

215

216 218

Romantic Venice

After the complete loss of its political dominance, in the wake of the fall of the Republic, the city seemed to close in on itself and search for its reason for existence in its own reflected image. In symbiosis with its watery mythology, the myth of Venice developed in this period; fostered by the Romantics, this myth is a melange of nostalgia for bygone splendor, and complacent musing on present decadence. In architecture, all of this is expressed in the "repechage" of repertories linked to the mythical eras of the city-state: the Veneto-Byzantine, the Lombardesque, the Flamboyant Gothic, revisited and adapted by various architects, including Meduna, Cadorin, Boito, a subspecies of new constructions or restoration. The city changed radically in its key areas: great hotels, banking headquarters, and insurance office buildings clustering around San Marco and Rialto.

Created from nothing, the Lido at the end of the century became the second arena for Romantic architecture: not oppressed by a direct confrontation with the past, the medieval revival here became the point of departure for personal forms of experimentation that were to lead to the art nouveau of Sullam and Torres, or the Orientalism of the Hotel Excelsior. Not only was it the destination of many international tourists, but it also became an industrial and shipping center: this second aspect, which became more distinct after Italian Unification, developed after 1880. Santa Marta and the Giudecca were to constitute its principal theaters, likewise endowed with a Romantic aura.

204

Neo-Gothic Building at Campo San Fantin
1846
Giovanni Battista Meduna
San Marco 1895, Campo San Fantin
Actv: Sant'Angelo or Santa Maria del Giglio vaporetto stop
This is the first example of the neo-medieval revival that appeared in Venice, formulated with a certain philological rigor. Although the composition is quite simple, the elevation overlooking the Campo reveals a series of references to local tradition, particular apparent in the central trefoils with inflected, three-lobe arches.
BIBLIOGRAPHY: *Romanelli 1977,* pp. 294 ff.; *Romanelli 1988,* pp. 290 ff.

205

Palazzo Giovannelli (or Giovanelli)
15th century, rebuilt in 1847-1848
Giovanni Battista Meduna
Cannaregio 2292, Strada Nuova
Actv: San Marcuola or Ca' d'Oro vaporetto stop
An exceptional encounter of Gothic and Neo-Gothic styles, the palazzo presents an elevation particularly rich in tracery motifs, overlooking the Rio di Noale. Restructured by Meduna during the restoration of Ca' d'Oro, the interiors show the influence of the medievalist style of the time, and this is particularly evident in the entryway and in the octagonal staircase.
BIBLIOGRAPHY: *Romanelli 1988,* pp. 299 ff.; *Romanelli 1990,* pp. 124 ff.

206

Caffè Florian
1858
Lodovico Cadorin
San Marco 56-59, Procuratie Nuove
Actv: San Marco or San Zaccaria vaporetto stop
The architect as well of the furnishings of the Caffè Quadri (located on the opposite side of the square, but modified in the meanwhile), Cadorin here seems to take inspiration from the decorative models of 18th-century Venice. There is a perceptible and elegant eclectic taste, dominating in the crystal mirrors and painted woods and bronze and mahogany treads.
BIBLIOGRAPHY: *Romanelli 1977,* pp. 314 ff.; *Pavanello-Romanelli 1983,* pp. 235 ff.

207
Palazzina Marioni near San Trovaso
1858
Lodovico Cadorin
Dorsoduro 1259, Rio di San Trovaso
Actv: Accademia vaporetto stop

Set at the intersection of two Rios, in sight of the Grand Canal, this building presents in the façades a dense terracotta decoration, punctuated here and there by items in white stone: arched lintels, and portals are made with formed terracotta tiles that borrow Lombardesque and Codussian motifs, revealing Cadorin's skills as a decorator.
BIBLIOGRAPHY: *Romanelli 1977, p. 307; Pavanello-Romanelli 1983, p. 243.*

208
Hotel Londra and Beau Rivage
1855, 1867
Carlo Ruffini, Giovanni Fuin
Castello 4171, Riva degli Schiavoni
Actv: San Zaccaria vaporetto stop

The difference between the right and the left section of what is now the Hotel Londra is quite significant; one was formulated in a measured Neo-Classicism (Ruffini), and the other in a proto-Renaissance language (Ruin); two different ways in which the city proposed its artistic history to the new but growing tourist trade.
BIBLIOGRAPHY: *Romanelli 1977, pp. 310 ff.*

209
Fondaco dei Turchi
13th century, rebuilt in 1869
Federico Berchet
Santa Croce 1730, Salizzada del Fontego
Actv: Riva di Biasio or San Stae vaporetto stop

Without Berchet's radical reconstruction, this would have been the most important Veneto-Byzantine civil structure. This palazzo, originally owned by the Pesaro family became, from 1575 on, an obligatory way station for Greek merchandise and merchants. From 1898 until 1922, it was the location of the Correr Museum, and it now houses the Museum of Natural History.
BIBLIOGRAPHY: *Calabi 1991/b, pp. 802 ff.*

210
Strada Nuova
1867-1871
Cannaregio

Actv: Ca' d'Oro or San Marcuola vaporetto stop

Long conceived as part of a rapid link between Rialto and the Railway Station, this traffic artery comprises two rectilinear portions converging on the Campo San Felice; the demolition required to give it its considerable girth was very extensive (it is about 10 meters wide), and this consti-tutes the first radical piece of modern urban planning in the city.

BIBLIOGRAPHY: *Romanelli 1977, pp. 422 ff.; Pavanello-Romanelli 1983, pp. 226 ff.*

211
Bacino Orseolo
1865-1914
San Marco 1164-1219

Actv: San Marco vaporetto stop

By various architects (including Federico Berchet and Giovanni Battista Meduna) was the plan to create a landing basin near Saint Mark's Square; the name comes from the Orseolo Hospice, later transformed into the Hotel Cavalletto. Around it stand principally banks and hotels; among the hotels is the Bonvecchiati, built in 1908-1914 by Nicolò Piamonte.

BIBLIOGRAPHY: *Romanelli 1977, p. 419 ff.; Pavanello-Romanelli 1983, pp. 226 ff.*

212
Calle Larga XXII Marzo
1874-1906
Francesco Balduin and others
San Marco 2032-2424

Actv: Santa Maria del Giglio or San Marco vaporetto stop

The urban plan of 1874 called for the widening and straightening of the Calle Lunga San Moisè. The architect, Francesco Balduin, proposed a single backdrop, such as the head-building in Neo-Lombardesque style (address street number 2032); despite the diversity of the structures, this was to give a homogenous appearance to the buildings along the new road.

BIBLIOGRAPHY: *Romanelli 1977, pp. 430 ff.; Pavanello-Romanelli 1983, p. 228*

213

Palazzo Cavalli Franchetti
15th century, rebuilt in 1878-1882
Camillo Boito, Carlo Matscheg, and Girolamo Manetti
San Marco 2847, Campo San Vidal
Actv: Accademia vaporetto stop

Many are the similarities with Palazzo Giovanelli, though clearly in a more spectacular setting and with greater expenditure of resources; aside from the original work of Meduna, we see here too an encounter between a late-Gothic shell and an interior remodelled according to the neo-medievalist style of the late 19th century. A particularly prominent element is the large staircase exhibited on the exterior through a series of iron fittings which Boito placed further back than the polyforate windows and the stone tracery; iron plays a major role on the elevation facing the Rio, as well, in the form of a corbel and a gallery with an industrial air. The building, however, is best known for the interior decoration, where sculptures, paintings, and furnishings comprise a whole.

BIBLIOGRAPHY: *Romanelli 1990*

214

City Cemetery
1872-1881
Annibale Forcellini
Island of San Michele
Actv: Cimitero vaporetto stop

This project was implemented after a long series of fruitless proposals and two competitions. After setting aside the idea of a monumental complex, the cemetery came into existence as a functional structure installed with some grace into the surrounding context: this can be seen in the horizontal layout, in the measured Gothic references, and in the use of green area.

BIBLIOGRAPHY: *Romanelli 1977, pp. 229 ff.; Pavanello-Romanelli 1983, p. 233*

215
Cotton Mill at Santa Marta
1883-1911
Dorsoduro 2196, Fondamenta Bari
Actv: Santa Marta or San Basilio vaporetto stop
This is the largest of the complexes built in the industrial area of the former Campo di Marte (as many as a thousand worked here). It developed over various phases, while still maintaining a single character not without grace. The massive walls are softened by terracotta trim. This is one of the buildings of the University Institute of Architecture.
BIBLIOGRAPHY: Mazzotta 1990/d, pp. 198 ff.

216
Mulino Stucky
1897-1920
Ernest Wullekopf
Giudecca 810-820, Fondamenta San Biagio
Actv: Sant'Eufemia vaporetto stop
Identified by the corner tower, this massive monument in Hanseatic Gothic style dominates the Canal of Giudecca becoming, especially for those who enter Venice by this route, one of the most characteristic features of the urban landscape. It served as a pasta mill and grain silo until 1954; now it seems condemned to ruin despite the numerous proposals for reuse.
BIBLIOGRAPHY: Howard 1980, pp. 223 ff.; Mazzotta 1990/e, pp. 200 ff.

217
Tobacco Manufactury
1786-1928
Santa Croce 423, Rio delle Burchielle
Actv: Piazzale Roma vaporetto stop
A number of renovations have been carried out over time, starting from the original nucleus built in the 18th century, identifiable in the part surrounding the entry portal. Particularly important to its appearance are the renovations done in the period around 1840-1850 (engineer, Giuseppe Mezzani); the covered bridge over the Rio, neo-medieval in style, dates back to the Twenties.
BIBLIOGRAPHY: Mazzotta 1990/c, pp. 194 ff.

218

Brewery at Giudecca
1909-1920
Consiglio Fano and Ugo Vigevano
Giudecca, Fondamenta San Biagio 801
Actv: Sant'Eufemia vaporetto stop

Amidst a complex in collapse, the central structure, formerly a distillery, stands out. It is a building crowned by merlons and embellished by a series of motifs that link it to the Mulino Stucky (such as the biforate windows inscribed within blind ogee arches). Rebuilt after 1980 by Giuseppe Gambirasio, it is now a residential complex.
BIBLIOGRAPHY: *Mazzotta* 1990/f, p. 203; *Polano* 1991, p. 226

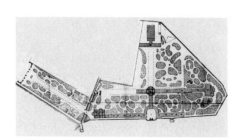

219

Site of the International Art Exposition
from 1887
Giardini di Castello
Actv: Giardini vaporetto stop

With the final renovation of the *motta* of Sant'Antonio, between Castello and Sant'Elena, the gardens of Selva were expanded (see entry no. 195); in this new area, the Venice Biennale has been held since 1895. The decision to build permanent national pavillions gave origin to a sort of village of the muses, with a sequence of significant but unconnected works of architecture (see entry no. 239).
BIBLIOGRAPHY: *Mulazzani* 1988; *Polano* 1991, pp. 218 ff.

220

Fish Market
1907
Cesare Laurenti and Domenico Rupolo
San Polo, Campo della Pescaria
Actv: Rialto or San Silvestro vaporetto stop

In replacing an iron and glass construction built in 1881, the building ended a long-running debate over the construction of a covered market in Pescaria. It takes the form of a medieval loggia, punctuated by oval arches; the architects claimed to have taken inspiration in its design from the paintings of Carpaccio.
BIBLIOGRAPHY: *Pavanello-Romanelli* 1983, p. 231

221

Hotel Excelsior at Lido
1898-1908
Giovanni Sardi
Lido, Lungomare Marconi 41

This is the first and the most significant hotel complex built at Lido, opened fifty years after the first bathing establishment. Sardi took his inspiration from the local traditions, especially the Veneto-Byzantine tradition, and mixed them with Moorish motifs. With an eye of consideration for his cosmopolitan clients, the true reference however is to the Grands Hotels of Cairo and the Côte d'Azur.

BIBLIOGRAPHY: *Maretto 1969*, pp. 61 ff.; *Pavanello-Romanelli 1983*, pp. 249 ff.

222

Hotel des Bains at Lido
1905-1909
Francesco Marsich
Lido, Lungomare Marconi 17

This was the first hotel built by CIGA, in far more cautious artistic forms than the nearby Excelsior; and yet the history of this hotel was inseparably linked to the history of Lido. Its fame – spread by film and literature – was linked much more to the celebrated *capanne* (small thatched huts) on the beach than to the conventional eclecticism of the façades.

BIBLIOGRAPHY: *Pavanello-Romanelli 1983*, p. 249

223

House by De Maria ("Tre Oci")
1910-1913
Mario De Maria
Giudecca, Fondamenta delle Zitelle
Actv: Zitelle vaporetto stop

This house/studio was designed by the owner, a painter. Here the Neo-Gothic references are only a point of departure, developed through curious combinations. This is true of the three large "eyes" that gave light to the atelier and from which the palazzo took its name and appearance.

BIBLIOGRAPHY: *Maretto 1969*, pp. 72 ff.; *Howard 1980*, p. 226

224

Palazzetto Stern near San Barnaba
1909-1912
Giuseppe Berti
Dorsoduro 2792/b, Calle del Traghetto
Actv: Ca' Rezzonico vaporetto stop
In terms of stylistic consistency, this may be the most significant Neo-Medieval piece of architecture of all those, designed *ex novo*, built on the Grand Canal. It presents itself as a total work of art in which every detail has been designed. The collaboration of the painter and decorator Raffaele Mainella seems to have been decisive to the Byzantine-style interior decoration.
BIBLIOGRAPHY: *Maretto 1969, p. 67*

225

Nardi's Houses at Corte dell'Alboro
1909-1914
Giulio Alessandri
San Marco 3883-87, Corte dell'Alboro
Actv: Sant'Angelo vaporetto stop
Of exceptional size and uniformity of expression, the great backdrop crafted by Alessandri creates an urban space all to itself in the fabric of the city; this happens despite the stylistic references wavering between Romantic and Veneto-Byzantine. In the imposing brick mass, there are integrated decorations inspired by art nouveau.
BIBLIOGRAPHY: *Pavanello-Romanelli 1983, p. 248*

226

Neo-Gothic Building at Zattere
1912-1914
Giuseppe Berti
Dorsoduro 1413, Zattere al ponte Longo
Actv: Zattere vaporetto stop
Along with the similar and contemporaneous Scarpa's house by Giovanni Sardi (address street number 1386), Berti's construction demonstrates the degree of transformation of which the neo-medieval architecture of the early 20th century was capable. It became a medium through which to express properly (and in a non-banal way) even themes of modern architecture, as in a residential building at the side of a road.
BIBLIOGRAPHY: *Pavanello-Romanelli 1983, p. 248*

227

House by Torres at Rio del Gaffaro
1905-1907
Giuseppe Torres
Dorsoduro 3544
Actv: Piazzale Roma vaporetto stop

This is perhaps the best known example of neo-medieval architecture; here Torres draws on a broad repertory that ranges from the Romantic to the Byzantine. With the assistance of the greenery and the location, the little villa therefore becomes an expression of an intimate and meditative poetics, more than the product of an erudite exercise.

BIBLIOGRAPHY: Nicoletti 1978, p. 256; Pavanello-Romanelli 1983, p. 245; Romanelli 1985/b

228

Commercial Building by Bacino Orseolo
1908-1910
San Marco 4410, Fondamenta Orseolo
Actv: San Marco vaporetto stop

This is considered to be the most significant among the buildings of a certain size of Venetian art nouveau. Here Sullam took on the challenge of a multi-story building; the only decoration that he imposes on the bare façade is that of the windows on the *piano nobile* – an intentionally deformed and contorted Ionic order.

BIBLIOGRAPHY: Howard 1980, p. 227; Romanelli 1985/a

229

Hunting Lodge at Valle Zappa
1923-1924
Duilio Torres
South Lagoon, Valle Zappa

It is difficult to establish the architectural antecedents and the stylistic references of this singular building, which stands in the wilderness and seems to have popped out of a Nordic fable. Torres, at any rate, shows that he is familiar with international styles, from the School of Amsterdam to the Viennese Secession.

BIBLIOGRAPHY: Polano 1991, p. 214

230

Villa Monplaisir at Lido

1906
Guido Costante Sullam
Lido, Gran Viale 14
Built for Nicolò Spada, founder of CIGA Hotels, this small villa is intended as an updated piece of art nouveau. In the asymmetrical composition, rich in respected references (Horta, Hoffmann) there are pieces of high craftsmanship executed in a number of different materials: wall decorations, wrought iron, porcelain, brass.
BIBLIOGRAPHY: *Nicoletti 1978, p. 257; Romanelli 1985/a*

231

House of the Pharmacist at Lido

1926-1927
Brenno del Giudice
Lido, Via Sandro Gallo 74
For this simple and yet refined piece of small-scale architecture, a great variety of stylistic categories have been mentioned: from Art Déco to neo-late-Baroque, from Novecento to late eclecticism. The building at any rate testifies to the persistence and vitality of the Romantic and historicist current in the period between the wars.
BIBLIOGRAPHY: *Bossaglia 1984, p. 20; Polano 1991, p. 214*

232

Public Housing Area at Sant'Elena

1924-1927
Paolo Bertanza and others
Actv: Sant'Elena vaporetto stop
The clear and insistent reference to local tradition is not limited to the façades, but above all to the urban layout. The blocks are arranged according to a number of different solutions, which generate recognizable spaces: Calli, courtyards, and Campielli which bear the names of battles from World War I.
BIBLIOGRAPHY: *Somma 1983, pp. 79 ff.; De Carli-Zaggia 1983, pp. 120 ff.; Romanelli 1985/a*

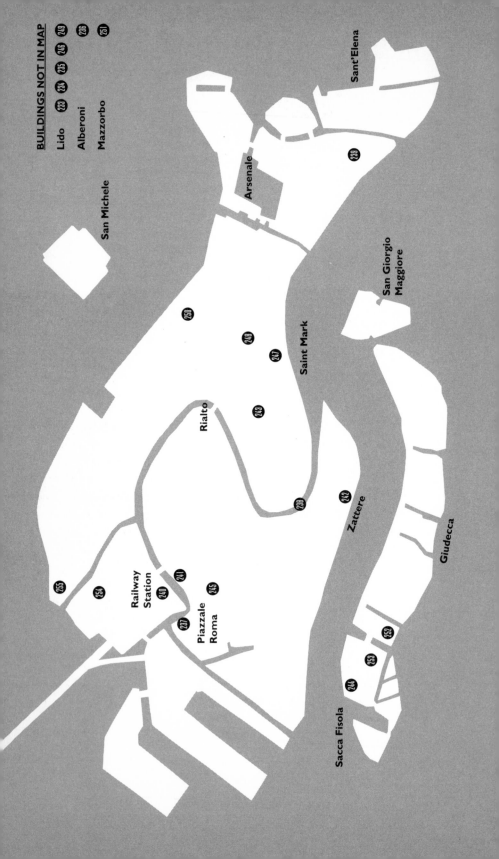

BUILDINGS NOT IN MAP

Lido ②③③ ②③④ ②③⑤ ②④⑥ ②④⑨

Alberoni ②③⑥

Mazzorbo ②⑤①

San Michele

Arsenale

②⑤⓪

②④⑧

②④⑦

Saint Mark

Rialto

②④⑨

②③⑧

San Giorgio Maggiore

②③⑨

Sant'Elena

Zattere ②④②

Giudecca

Railway Station

②⑤⑤

②⑤④

②④⓪ ②④①

②③⑦

Piazzale Roma ②④⑤

Sacca Fisola ②④④

②⑤③

②⑤②

Venice and Modern Architecture

The relationship between Venice and modern architecture is not a simple one, and it is perhaps best known for the opportunities missed than for the works built – suffice it to think of the projects by Wright, Le Corbusier, and Kahn that were turned down.

At first the Lido constituted a free zone, set aside for experimentation; it was here that the first white architecture sprang up, associated with images of life in the open air. Amidst the stones of Venice, the most spectacular stylistic intrusions were those tied to infrastructures and their points of arrival in the city: the giant parking garage in Piazzale Roma, the railroad station, and the airport located at Lido. Otherwise, the new structures seem to be encapsulated inside enclosures, and were not visible from outside: in the citadel of the Biennale and in the interior decorating and architecture of Scarpa. Alongside all of this, which reeks of conflict, there is another approach, the most common in the postwar period: it is the search for a compromise with the image of the city and its existing environmental features. Ideally, that is the spirit of the design of Gardella for the Zattere, and, in more recent times, a series of plans for residential complexes. In material terms, they are located in the areas left undeveloped after the dismantling of port structures and industrial manufacturing – these marginal zones, and no longer Lido, today constitute the area of experimentation.

233

Heliotherapic Hospital at Lido
1922-1923
Duilio Torres
Lido, Via Alberoni

This is considered to be the first expression of modern architecture in Venice; as such it was presented at the Stuttgart Exposition in 1927. With its great glass surfaces, set in diminishing sequences in order to optimize their exposure to the sun, this building also appeared as a non-provincial reflection of the most up-to-date rationalist developments.

BIBLIOGRAPHY: *Maraini 1928; Maretto 1969, p. 84*

234

Airport at Lido
1934
G. Cicogna
Lido, San Nicolò

Built in record time by the Provincial Government, this building had all of the trappings of the avant-garde from the outset. In the cunning assembly of features from the modernist repertoire, there are several significant elements – the glass tower at the center, and at one end, the semicircular ramp.

BIBLIOGRAPHY: *Le Tre Venezie 1935.*

235

Palazzo del Cinema at Lido
1937 and 1952
L. Guagliata and Angelo Scattolin
Lido, Lungomare Marconi

This building houses the offices and theatres of the International Film Festival, which began in 1932. Despite the explicit references to the modern style, it has a symmetrical and sober monumental form. The atrium, added in 1952, has upset the original equilibrium. This building is no longer sufficient for the requirements of the Exposition, and in 1990-1991 a competition was held for new proposals.

BIBLIOGRAPHY: *Maretto 1969, p. 102*

236

Seaside Health Resort at Alberoni
1936-1937
Daniele Calabi and Antonio Salce
Alberoni, Via Comunale
This project was much praised by the critics at the time. In the building, which is horizontally oriented, we see the features of a standard theme of the Thirties, used and developed – the solarium, portico, and dormitories with large windows on the exterior. The designers placed them within the Cartesian context of a square courtyard.
BIBLIOGRAPHY: *Avon 1992, pp. 29 ff., 38 ff.*

237

INA Parking Garage
1931-1934
Eugenio Miozzi
Actv: Piazzale Roma vaporetto stop
Visible from a distance, this giant garage has attained the role of a new city gate, the natural complement to the Littorio automobile bridge, now called Liberty bridge. The large horizontal bands characterize an elevation in which there are no mediations with the traditional image of Venice.
BIBLIOGRAPHY: *Nebbia 1934; Polano 1991, p. 220*

238

Accademia Bridge
1932
Eugenio Miozzi
Actv: Accademia vaporetto stop
This bridge replaced a cast iron bridge from the time of Austrian occupation. Made of wood, the new structure was at first meant only as a temporary replacement, while a competition was held for architectural proposals. In realty, its slender structure is now part of the urban landscape. In fact, in 1983-1984 it was thoroughly restored.
BIBLIOGRAPHY: *Maretto 1969, pp. 94 ff.*

239

Pavilions of the Biennale
from 1895 on
Castello, Giardini di Castello

Actv: Giardini vaporetto stop

The individual national pavilions, mostly built between 1930 and 1965, accentuate the idea of something extraneous from its location, separated from the city not only by the water (see entry no. 219). Many of these buildings reflect significant and poetic work by great masters of architecture: let us mention in particular the Austrian pavilion (J. Hoffmann, 1934), the Dutch pavilion (G.T. Rietveld, 1954), and the Finnish pavilion (A. Aalto, 1956). There are many projects by Carlo Scarpa, though many of these have been heavily altered: the ticket window (1948), the Venezuelan pavilion (1954), and part of the unrecognizable Italian pavilion which, after the international competition of 1988, will be (we hope) rebuilt by Francesco Cellini. Lastly, the book pavilion, by James Stirling (1991).

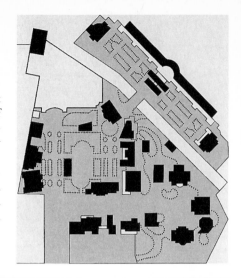

BIBLIOGRAPHY: Maretto 1969, p. 77 ff.; Mulazzani 1988

240

Railway Station
1952-1955
Paolo Perilli and Ufficio Tecnico delle Ferrovie dello Stato
Cannaregio, Fondamenta Santa Lucia

Actv: Stazione vaporetto stop

This building was erected twenty years after a competition for plans and ideas (1934), which remained on the drawing board. After Piazzale Roma, the other gate to Venice takes a radically different approach from the previous structure; punctuated horizontally, the long elevation made of Istrian stone constitutes the only radically modern feature on the Grand Canal.

BIBLIOGRAPHY: Maretto 1969, pp. 97 ff.; Facchinelli 1987, pp. 237 ff.

241

INAIL Headquarters
1952-1956
Giuseppe Samonà and Egle Trincanato
Santa Croce 712, Calle Nova San Simon
Actv: Stazione vaporetto stop
Almost directly across from the new station stands this office building, and its architects did nothing to conceal its function; here too there are no inhibitions about the past. As such, this building is part of a series of buildings for the service industry that, in the Fifties, were constructed in the empty areas between the railway station and Piazzale Roma.
BIBLIOGRAPHY: *Polano 1991, p. 220*

242

House at Zattere
1954-1958
Ignazio Gardella
Dorsoduro 401, Zattere allo Spirito Santo
Actv: Zattere vaporetto stop
This is perhaps the best known of all the instances of modern architecture set in the heart of historical Venice; it is precisely the relationship with the architectural and environmental context that gives this projects its *raison d'être*, which drew praise and criticism in equal measure. It is certain that here Gardella adopts forms and styles to the local situation that are totally extraneous from it, such as the residential apartment block.
BIBLIOGRAPHY: *Argan 1959, pp. 163 ff.; Morresi 1992*

243

Main Offices of the Cassa di Risparmio
1964-1971
Angelo Scattolin with Pier Luigi Nervi
San Marco 4216, Campo Manin
Actv: Sant'Angelo or Rialto vaporetto stop
This project underwent a lengthy gestation, due chiefly to problems of structural engineering (hence the consultation of Nervi, which resulted in the light ribbing on the lower floors). In the elevations, crossed by a rectangular grid, there is an inversion of roles between the glassed basement and the upper section in stone.
BIBLIOGRAPHY: *Maretto 1969, p. 129; Howard 1980, p. 234*

244

INA CASA development at Sacca Fisola
1958-1967
Ufficio Tecnico IACP
Actv: Sacca Fisola vaporetto stop

The largest publicly funded development in insular Venice; this is an ideal urbanistic continuation of the villages that had just previously been built on the shores of the lagoon at San Giuliano. The buildings, of varying height, are apparently inspired by a moderate environmentalism, which can be seen chiefly in the irregular arrangement of the volumes.

BIBLIOGRAPHY: *De Carli-Zaggia 1983, pp. 132 ff.*

245

University Institute of Architecture
1956-1958
Daniele Calabi and M. Bacci
Santa Croce 191, Campazzo dei Tolentini
Actv: Piazzale Roma vaporetto stop

This renovation chiefly concerns the interiors where, in part through the use of new technologies, large spaces have been created for teaching. On the exterior, on the other hand, the structure and appearance of a courtyard building has been maintained, set around the quadriporticus. The 1985 version of the entry was designed by Carlo Scarpa.

BIBLIOGRAPHY: *Dalla Costa 1992/b; Franco-Zucconi 1992*

246

House by Calabi at Lido
1961-1963
Daniele Calabi
Lido, Piazza Fiume 1

Conceived as an architect's home and studio, this small palazzo facing the Lungomare acquired its forms from the villa that stood here previously. Although it is hidden amidst the greenery, it shows features that distinguish it from the similar structures that surround it – in particular, between the roof and the curtain wall in terracotta, the glassed surface of the attic floor stands out.

BIBLIOGRAPHY: *Calabi-Folin 1968; Dalla Costa 1992/b*

247

Olivetti Showroom in Saint Mark's Square
1957-1958
Carlo Scarpa
San Marco 101, Procuratie Vecchie
Actv: San Marco vaporetto stop
This has been called by some a "masterpiece of contemporary architecture." With its long, narrow shape, the showroom gives a good idea of Scarpa's skill at organizing interior space and integrating it with the materials used; arranged according to refined and original concepts, the materials become the protagonists of the environment, vibrant with light.
BIBLIOGRAPHY: *Dal Co-Mazzariol* 1984, p. 120; *Marcianò* 1984, pp. 70 ff.

248

Querini-Stampalia Foundation
1961-1963
Carlo Scarpa
Castello 4794, Rio di Santa Maria Formosa
Actv: Rialto or San Zaccaria vaporetto stop
Scarpa's work here stopped at the ground floor and includes the construction of the new entry atrium, a hall for exhibitions, and an interior garden, conceived in the form of a *hortus conclusus*. Remarkable here is the invention of the walkways, along the water, which Scarpa has penetrate the building itself, in close conversation with the stone.
BIBLIOGRAPHY: *Dal Co-Mazzariol* 1984, p. 124; *Marcianò* 1984, pp. 112 ff.

249

Yacht Club and Residence at Lido
1979-1981
Iginio Cappai and Pietro Mainardis
Lido, Lungomare Marconi 52
Immediately after the Orientalist "deliriums" of Sardi, we see these two sharp and clear white volumes, arranged along the beach. This is a "dependence" of the Hotel Excelsior, and they form a row with a line of small apartment buildings and another building, built to house the offices of the yachting club.
BIBLIOGRAPHY: *Gregotti* 1981; *Polano* 1991, p. 216

250

Expansion of the City Hospital
from 1978 on
Luciano Semerani and Gigetta Tamaro
Castello, Campo Santi Giovanni e Paolo
Actv: Ospedale o Fondamente Nuove vaporetto stop

After discarding the idea of a new hospital in San
Giobbe, designed by Le Corbusier in 1964, a
program of renovation and expansion of the
ancient cloister structure was undertaken. This
row building, intended for recovering patients,
is based on a modular form which can be
repeated, and is distinguished by a barrel-vault
roof not unlike that of the Church of the Miracoli.
BIBLIOGRAPHY: *Domus 1987; Polano 1991, p. 224*

251

Development of Low-Income Housing at Mazzorbo
1979-1986
Giancarlo De Carlo and assistants
Island of Mazzorbo
Actv: Mazzorbo vaporetto stop

In the volumetric composition, in the use of
colors, and in several structural details, we can
clearly see references to the architecture of the
island of Burano, of which this constitutes an
expansion. The residential blocks are arranged
along a straight central axis which is evocative of
other images and other architectural models.
BIBLIOGRAPHY: *Magnani-Val 1985, p. 60; Polano 1991,
p. 216*

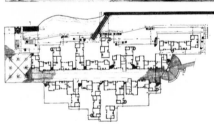

252

IACP Complex at the Giudecca
1980-1986
Gino Valle and assistants
Sacca Fisola, Canale dei Lavraneri
Actv: Sant'Eufemia or Sacca Fisola vaporetto stop

Behind the Mulino Stucky, this structure makes
use of elevations that heretofore were quite
marginal – on two opposite canals, we see a
sequence of close-set modules that borrow
motifs from local architecture. On the interior,
we see a different approach, with a dominance
of references to functionalist architecture, within
a very orderly grid.
BIBLIOGRAPHY: *Magnani-Val 1985, p. 80; Croset 1986*

253
Residential Complex at Sacca Fisola
1982-1989
Iginio Cappai, Pietro Mainardis, and Valeriano Pastor
Sacca Fisola, Area Fregnan
Actv: Sacca Fisola vaporetto stop

These are two separate structures arranged around a square courtyard. Of particular interest is the relationship with the water, which penetrates the ground floor set on pilings, creating spaces for mooring boats. Marked by strips of white stone, the colourful elevations hearken back to non-vernacular instances of traditional Venetian architecture.
BIBLIOGRAPHY: *De Michelis 1986; Polano 1991, p. 228*

254
Public Housing in the Former Saffa Area at San Giobbe
1984-1989
Vittorio Gregotti and assistants
Cannaregio 469 ff., Campiello Ca' Pesaro
Actv: Tre Archi vaporetto stop

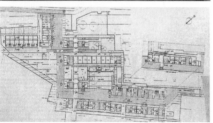

In the architecture of the elevations, of an elementary type, the covered roof-terraces alone restore a tie to tradition. In this work of industrialized architecture the relationship is contextual in nature; in other words, it is linked to the form and quality of the urban spaces that it is intended to stitch together and recreate.
BIBLIOGRAPHY: *Magnani-Val 1985, pp. 35 ff.; Ranzani 1989*

255
Public Housing at the Sacca San Girolamo
1987-1990
F. Bortoluzzi and the City Urban Planning Office
Cannaregio 800 ff., Fondamenta di Cannaregio
Actv: Tre Archi vaporetto stop

Looking out over the lagoon, alongside the slaughterhouse of San Giobbe and therefore clearly visible from the bridge across the lagoon, this development of 47 residences takes its inspiration from models in the local tradition. The large chimneys shaped like funnels, which dominate its silhouette, announce an interior organization based on closed courtyards similar to Campielli.
BIBLIOGRAPHY: *Bauwelt 1993*

Bibliography

The year and/or city of the consulted edition is indicated within brackets whenever different from the first.

1502
M.A. SABELLICO, *Del sito di Venezia città*, Venice (1985).

1524-28
PH. DE COMMYNES, *Memoires*, Paris.

1663
F. SANSOVINO, *Venetia, città nobilissima et singolare*, Venice (1968).

1703
L. CARLEVARIJS, *Le fabriche, e vedute, di Venezia, disegnate, poste in prospettiva et intagliate, con privilegii*, Venice.

1735
A. VISENTINI, *Prospectus Magni Canalis Venetiarum*, Venice (Milan, 1987).

1786
J.W. GOETHE, *Viaggio in Italia* (Milan 1983).

1838-40
L. CICOGNARA, A. DIEDO, G.A. SELVA, *Le fabbriche più cospicui di Venezia...*, Venice.

1865
H. TAINE, *Voyage en Italie*, Paris.

1928
A. MARAINI, "L'architettura e le arti decorative alla XVI Biennale veneziana", *Architettura e arti decorative*, II, 2.

1931
G. FOGOLARI, *I Frari e i Santi Giovanni e Paolo*, Milan.

1934
U. NEBBIA, "Autorimessa a Venezia", *Casa bella*, no. 83.

1935
"La nuova stazione all'aeoporto di Venezia", *Le Tre Venezie*, redazionale, July.

1936
G. LORENZETTI, *Ca' Rezzonico*, Venice.

1939
S. BETTINI, *Aspetti bizantineggianti dell'architettura di Torcello*, in G. Fiocco, F. Forlati (editors), Torcello, Venice.
F. FORLATI, *L'architettura a Torcello*, in G. Fiocco, F. Forlati (editors), Torcello, Venice.

1941
M. BRUNETTI, M. DAZZI, *Il Fondaco nostro dei Tedeschi*, Venice.

1946
S. BETTINI, *L'architettura di S. Marco (origine e significato)*, Padua.

1948
E. TRINCANATO, *Venezia minore*, Milan.

1949
A. SARTORI, *Guida storico-artistica della Basilica di S. Maria Gloriosa dei Frari*, Padua.

1950
G. MARIACHER, *Il Palazzo Ducale di Venezia*, Florence.
G. MARIACHER, T. PIGNATTI, *La Basilica di S. Marco in Venezia*, Florence.

1953
M. MURARO, *Nuova guida di Venezia e delle sue isole*, Florence.

1954
C. SEMENZATO, *L'architettura di Baldassarre Longhena*, Padua.

1959
G.C. ARGAN, *Ignazio Gardella*, Milan.

1960
O. DEMUS, *The Church of San Marco in Venice*, Washington D.C.

1961

L. ANGELINI, Bartolomeo Bono e Guglielmo d'Alzano. Architetti bergamaschi in Venezia, Bergamo.

S. TRAMONTIN, S. Stae, la chiesa e la parrocchia, Venice.

1962

E. BASSI, Architettura del Sei e Settecento a Venezia, Naples.

S. TRAMONTIN, S. Maria Mater Domini, Venice.

R. WITTKOWER, Le chiese di Andrea Palladio e l'architettura barocca veneta, in V. Branca (editor), Barocco europeo e barocco veneziano, Venice.

1963

G. LORENZETTI, Venezia e il suo estuario, Venice (1st ed. 1926).

1964

S. BETTINI, Le origini di Venezia, Florence.

A.M. CACCIN, La Basilica dei Santi Giovanni e Paolo, Venice.

C. SEMENZATO, "Pietro e Tullio Lombardo architetti", Bollettino C.I.S.A., VI.

R. WITTKOWER, Principi architettonici nell'età dell'Umanesimo, Turin.

1965

G. MARIACHER, Palazzo Vendramin-Calergi, Venice.

A. NIERO, La chiesa dei Carmini, Venice.

F. ZAVA BOCCAZZI, La Basilica dei Santi Giovanni e Paolo, Venice.

1966

D.L. GARDANI, "La chiesa di San Giacomo di Rialto", Venezia sacra, no. 6.

A. MASSARI, "Giorgio Massari e la facciata della chiesa della Pietà", Ateneo veneto, no. 4.

G.G. ZORZI, Le chiese e i ponti di Andrea Palladio, Vicenza.

1968

D. CALABI, M. FOLIN, "Le ultime opere di Daniele Calabi", in Architettura. Cronache e storia, no. 150.

1969

P. MARETTO, Venezia, Genova.

P. MURRAY, Architettura del Rinascimento, Milan.

M. TAFURI, Jacopo Sansovino e l'architettura del '500 a Venezia, Padua.

1970

E. ARSLAN, Venezia gotica. L'architettura civile gotica veneziana, Milan.

M. MURARO, Palazzo Contarini a San Beneto, Venice.

E. TRINCANATO, Il Palazzo Ducale, in AA.VV., Piazza San Marco. L'architettura, la storia, le funzioni, Padua.

1971

A. MASSARI, Giorgio Massari. Architetto veneziano del Settecento, Venice.

L. PUPPI, Michele Sanmicheli architetto di Verona, Padua.

1972

J. ACKERMAN, Palladio, Turin.

G. ROMANELLI, "Architetti e architetture a Venezia tra Otto e Novecento", in Antichità viva, no. 5.

1973

R. CEVESE, L'opera del Palladio, in AA.VV., Palladio, catalogue of the exhibition, Milan.

M. MURARO, "Il tempio votivo di Santa Maria della Salute in un poema del Seicento", Ateneo veneto, XI.

L. PUPPI, Andrea Palladio, 2 vol., Milan.

1974

T. MANGINI, I teatri di Venezia, Milan.

1975

D. HOWARD, Jacopo Sansovino. Architecture and Patronage in Renaissance Venice, New Haven and London.

1976

E. BASSI, Palazzi di Venezia. Admiranda urbis Venetae, Venice.

U. FRANZOI, D. DI STEFANO, Le chiese di Venezia, Venice.

R. MASOBELLO, M. TARLÀ, L'architettura di Palazzo Pisani, in Il conservatorio di musica Benedetto Marcello, Venice.

1977

L. PUPPI, L. OLIVATO, Mauro Codussi e l'architettura veneziana del primo Rinascimento, Milan.

G. ROMANELLI, Venezia Ottocento, Rome.

G. VIO, "I 'mistri' della chiesa di San Fantin in Venezia", Arte veneta, XXI.

1978

E. BASSI, L'Accademia, in Venezia nell'età di Canova, 1780-1830, catalogue of the exhibition, Venice.

S. BETTINI, Venezia. Nascita di una città, Milan.

M. NICOLETTI, L'architettura liberty in Italia, Rome-Bari.

G. ROMANELLI (1978/a), La città: architettura e servizi, in Venezia nell'età di Canova, 1780-1830, catalogue of the exhibition, Venice.

G. ROMANELLI (1978/b), Urbanistica e architettura negli anni napoleonici dagli interventi all'insegnamento accademico, in Venezia nell'età di Canova, 1780-1830, catalogue of the exhibition, Venice.

1979

M. VECCHI, Santa Fosca, origini prebizantine, in Torcello. Ricerche, contributi, Rome.

1980

M. BRUSATIN, Venezia nel Settecento: stato, architettura, territorio, Turin.

D. HOWARD, The Architectural History of Venice, London.

M. TAFURI, "Sapienza di stato" e "atti mancati": architettura e tecnica urbana nella Venezia del Cinquecento, in L. Puppi (editor), Architettura e utopia nella Venezia del Cinquecento, catalogue of the exhibition, Milan.

1981

V. FONTANA, "Camillo Boito e il restauro a Venezia", Casabella, no. 472.

V. GREGOTTI, "Megasegno in laguna", Domus, no. 617.

S. LUNARDON, Le Zitelle, in L. Puppi (editor), Palladio e Venezia, Florence.

T. PIGNATTI (editor), Le scuole di Venezia, Milan.

1982

S. BIADENE, Catalogo delle opere, in S. Biadene, L. Puppi (editors), Longhena, catalogue of the exhibition, Milan.

R. LIEBERMAN, L'Architettura del Rinascimento a Venezia 1450-1540, Florence.

E. MARTINELLI, F. PEDROCCO, T. PIGNATTI, Palazzo Labia a Venezia, Turin.

M. TAFURI, Ricerca del Rinascimento. Principi, città, architetti, Turin.

1983

E. CONCINA, La macchina territoriale. La progettazione della difesa nel Cinquecento veneto, Rome-Bari.

L. DE CARLI, M. ZAGGIA, Tipologie edilizie e qualità architettonica, in E. Barbiani (editor), Edilizia popolare a Venezia, Milan.

A. FOSCARI, M. TAFURI, L'armonia e i conflitti. La chiesa di San Francesco della Vigna nella Venezia del '500, Turin.

G. LORENZONI, Venezia medievale, tra Oriente e Occidente, in Storia dell'arte italiana, I vol., Dal Medioevo al Quattrocento, Turin.

J. MC ANDREW, L'architettura veneziana del primo Rinascimento, Venice.

G. PAVANELLO, G. ROMANELLI, Venezia nell'Ottocento. Immagini e mito, catalogue of the exhibition, Milan.

P. SOMMA (editor), Venezia nuova. La politica della casa 1893-1941, Venice.

1984

R. BOSSAGLIA, L'Art déco, Rome-Bari.

D. CALABI, P. MORACHIELLO, Rialto 1514-1538, gli anni della ricostruzione, in M. Tafuri (editor), "Renovatio urbis". Venezia nell'età di Andrea Gritti (1523-38), Rome.

E. CONCINA (1984/a), Fra Oriente e Occidente: gli Zen, un palazzo e il mito di Trebisonda, in M. Tafuri (editor), "Renovatio urbis". Venezia nell'età di Andrea Gritti (1523-1538), Rome.

E. CONCINA (1984/b), L'Arsenale della Repubblica di Venezia, Milan.

F. DAL CO, G. MAZZARIOL, Carlo Scarpa 1906-1978, Milan.

G. GIANIGHIAN, P. PAVANINI, Dietro i palazzi. Tre secoli di architettura minore a Venezia 1492-1803, catalogue of the exhibition, Venice.

A.F. MARCIANÒ, Carlo Scarpa, Bologna.

R. POLACCO, La cattedrale di Torcello, Treviso.

1985

A. ALBERTINI, L'architettura, in AA.VV., Palazzo Loredan e l'Istituto Veneto di Scienze, Lettere ed Arti, Venice.

S. BIADENE (1985/a), L'Accademia di Belle Arti, in L. Puppi, G. Romanelli, Le Venezie possibili. Da Palladio a Le Corbusier, catalogue of the exhibition, Milan.

S. BIADENE (1985/b), L'Ala Napoleonica, in L. Puppi, G. Romanelli, Le Venezie possibili. Da Palladio a Le Corbusier, Milan

D. CALABI, P. MORACHIELLO, "La questione della 'novitas' nella rifabbrica di San Giovanni Ele-

mosinario a Rialto", in Rassegna, no. 22.

C. MAGNANI, P.A. VAL (editors), "Venezia città del moderno", Rassegna, no. 22, monographic issue.

C. MANGO, Architettura bizantina, Milan 1978.

G.M. PILO, La chiesa dello "spedaletto" in Venezia, Venice.

G. ROMANELLI (1985/a), "Nuova edilizia veneziana all'inizio del XX secolo", Rassegna, no. 22.

G. ROMANELLI (1985/b), Il segno secessionista di Giuseppe Torres, in L. PUPPI, G. ROMANELLI, Le Venezie possibili. Da Palladio a Le Corbusier, catalogue of the exhibition, Milan.

G. ROMANELLI, Lido: gli anni del "Modernismo", in L. Puppi, G. Romanelli, Le Venezie possibili. Da Palladio a Le Corbusier, catalogue of the exhibition, Milan 1985.

M. TAFURI, Venezia e il Rinascimento, Turin.

1986

P.A. CROSET, "Sul progetto di Valle alla Giudecca", Lotus International, no. 51.

M. DE MICHELIS, "Nuovi progetti alla Giudecca. Tipi, edificazione e morfologia dell'isola", Lotus International, no. 51.

R. KRAUTHEIMER, Architettura paleocristiana e bizantina, Turin.

P. MARETTO, La casa veneziana nella storia della città dalle origini all'Ottocento, 2 vol., Venice.

G. ROMANELLI, G. PAVANELLO, Palazzo Grassi. Storia, architettura, decorazioni dell'ultimo palazzo veneziano, Venice.

G. VIO, "Nella cerchia del Longhena", Arte veneta, XL.

1987

M. BRUSATIN, G. PAVANELLO, Il Teatro la Fenice. I progetti, l'architettura, le decorazioni, Venice.

D. CALABI, Le fabbriche, in D. Calabi, P. Morachiello, *Rialto: le fabbriche e il Ponte 1514-1591*, Turin.

"Semerani, Tamaro. Il nuovo ospedale a Venezia", *Domus*, no. 688.

L. FACCHINELLI, *Il ponte ferroviario in laguna*, Venice.

P. MORACHIELLO, *Il Ponte*, in D. Calabi, P. Morachiello, *Rialto: le fabbriche e il Ponte 1514-1591*, Turin.

1988

M. BRUSATIN, *Il giardino della mente: immagine, luogo, non luogo*, in M. Azzi Visentini (editor), *Il giardino veneto. Storia e conservazione*, Milan.

E. CONCINA, *Una fabbrica "in mezzo della città": la chiesa e il convento di San Salvador*, in *Progetto San Salvador*, Venice.

M. MULAZZANI, *I padiglioni della Biennale. Venezia 1887-1988*, Milan.

G. ROMANELLI, *Venezia Ottocento. L'architettura, l'urbanistica*, Venice.

1989

B. AIKEMA, D. MEIJERS, *Nel regno dei poveri. Arte e storia dei grandi ospedali in età moderna 1474-1797*, Venice.

E. CONCINA, *Venezia nell'età moderna. Struttura e funzioni*, Venice.

R. PELLEGRITI, "La chiesa dell'ospedale di San Lazzaro dei Mendicanti", *Arte veneta*, XLIII.

E. RANZANI, "Gregotti Associati. Quartiere residenziale area ex-Saffa, Venezia", *Domus*, no. 704.

A. ZORZI, P. MARTON, *I palazzi veneziani*, Udine.

1990

U. FRANZOI, *Architettura*, in U. Franzoi, T. Pignatti, W. Wolters, *Il Palazzo Ducale di Venezia*, Treviso.

M. GEMIN, F. PEDROCCO, *Ca' Vendramin Calergi*, Milan.

D. MAZZOTTA (1990/a), *Il macello comunale di Venezia*, in F. Man-

cuso (editor), *Archeologia industriale nel Veneto*, Milan.

D. MAZZOTTA (1990/b), *I magazzini del sale*, in F. Mancuso (editor), *Archeologia industriale nel Veneto*, Milan.

D. MAZZOTTA (1990/c), *La manifattura tabacchi*, in F. Mancuso (editor), *Archeologia industriale nel Veneto*, Milan.

D. MAZZOTTA (1990/d), *Il cotonificio veneziano*, in F. Mancuso (editor), *Archeologia industriale nel Veneto*, Milan.

D. MAZZOTTA (1990/e), *Il Mulino Stucky*, in F. Mancuso (editor), *Archeologia industriale nel Veneto*, Milan.

D. MAZZOTTA (1990/f), *La birreria alla Giudecca*, in F. Mancuso (editor), *Archeologia industriale nel Veneto*, Milan.

G. ROMANELLI, *Tra gotico e neo-gotico. Palazzo Cavalli Franchetti a San Vidal*, Venice.

1991

D. CALABI (1991/a), *Il ghetto e la città*, in E. Concina, U. Camerino, D. Calabi, *La città degli Ebrei. Il ghetto di Venezia: architettura e urbanistica*, Venice.

D. CALABI (1991/b), *Magazzini, fondaci, dogane*, in *Storia di Venezia*, vol. XII, *Il mare*, edited by A. Tenenti, U. Tucci, Rome.

E. CONCINA, *Parva Jerusalem*, in E. Concina, U. Camerino, D. Calabi, *La città degli Ebrei. Il ghetto di Venezia: architettura e urbanistica*, Venice.

M. CUNICO, *Il giardino veneziano*, Venice.

S. POLANO, *Guida all'architettura italiana del Novecento*, Venice.

1992

A. AVON, *Opere pubbliche nel Veneto fascista (1933-38)*, in G. Zucconi (editor), *Daniele Calabi. Architetture e progetti 1932-1964*, catalogue of the exhibition, Venice.

M. DALLA COSTA (1992/a), *La casa studio al Lido di Venezia*, in G. Zucconi (editor), *Daniele Calabi. Architetture e progetti 1932-1964*, catalogue of the exhibition, Venice.

M. DALLA COSTA (1992/b), *Il restauro dei Tolentini e la nuova sede IUAV*, in G. Zucconi (editor), *Daniele Calabi. Architetture e progetti 1932-1964*, catalogue of the exhibition, Venice.

U. FRANZO, G. ZUCCONI, *Il restauro dei Tolentini: cronologia di un intervento*, in G. Zucconi (editor), *Daniele Calabi. Architetture e progetti 1932-1964*, catalogue of the exhibition, Venice.

M. MORRESI, *Casa alle Zattere*, in F. Buzzi Ceriani (editor), *Ignazio Gardella. Progetti e architetture 1933-1990*, catalogue of the exhibition, Venice.

M. TAFURI, *Ricerca del Rinascimento. Principi, città, architetti*, Turin.

1993

Bauwelt, currently being printed.

P. BRAUNSTEIN (editor), *Venise 1500*, Paris.

Undated

M. DA CANAL, *Les estoires de Venise, Cronaca veneziana in lingua francese dalle origini al 1275*, Venice (edited by A. Limentani, Florence, 1972).

Index of places

The names in small capital letters poit out to those edifices
which are extensively covered by the guide-book.
The bold faced numbers refer to the progressive numbers of the files.

Index of names

Photo credits

The bold faced numbers refer to the captions
and the rounded ones to the files on the building.

Archivio Fotografico Arsenale Editrice, Venice **1**,
9, **10**, 1, 12, 14, 15, 25, 35, 48, 49, 58-60,
63, 64, 74, 80, 85, 90, 93-98, 107, 111,
112, 115, 117, 121, 123, 125, 127, 132,
148-150, 153-155, 166, 167, 174, 178, 182,
186, 187, 191, 194, 209, 229, 254, 240
Archivio Fotografico Osvaldo Böhm, Venice 3-5,
7, 9, 10, 20-23, 26, 27, 31-34, 36, 40, 42,
44, 45, 47, 51-53, 55, 57, 61, 62, 65, 66,
68, 70, 71, 78, 79, 81, 86-89, 92, 99, 101,
103, 105, 106, 114, 116, 118, 120, 126,
129, 131, 133, 135, 137, 138, 140, 142,
146, 151, 156-159, 160, 163-165, 169,
170, 172, 173, 175-177, 181, 184, 185,
188, 192, 193, 196, 198-207, 210-213,
218, 220, 224
ASAC (Historical Archives of Contemporary Arts of
the Venice Biennale), Venice 219, 239
Donatella Calabi 236, 246
Cameraphoto, Venezia **11**
Correr Museum, Venice **5**
Michele Crosera, Venice 2, 6, 8, 11, 13, 16-19,
24, 28-30, 37-39, 41, 43, 46, 50, 54, 56,
67, 69, 72, 73, 75-77, 82-84, 91, 100, 102,
104, 108-110, 113, 119, 122, 124, 128,
130, 134, 136, 139, 141, 143-145, 147,
152, 161, 162, 168, 171, 179, 180, 183,
189, 190, 195, 197, 208, 214-217, 221-
223, 225-228, 230-235, 237, 238, 241-245,
247-252
Slides Archives of the History of Architecture
Department of IUAV, Venice **2-4**, **6-8**, **12-15**
Edilvenezia 255
Valeriano Pastor 253